Once Below a Time

Memories of Growing Up
in Rural Virginia at Mid-Century

Glynn Baugher

ONCE BELOW A TIME
MEMORIES OF GROWING UP IN RURAL VIRGINIA AT MID-CENTURY

iUniverse books may be ordered through booksellers or by contacting:

iUniverse
1663 Liberty Drive
Bloomington, IN 47403
www.iuniverse.com
1-800-Authors (1-800-288-4677)

ISBN: 978-1-5320-5937-7 (sc)
ISBN: 978-1-5320-5939-1 (hc)
ISBN: 978-1-5320-5938-4 (e)

Library of Congress Control Number: 2018912940

Print information available on the last page.

iUniverse rev. date: 10/29/2018

Dedication

This book is dedicated to my readers,
all of them, fit audience though few.

Prologue

This memoir grew out of a conversation I had with my dear, dear college friend and three-year roommate, Paul Phillips, at what was then Addison's Restaurant at Emory and Henry College. Conversation between us almost never flags, and when it does, the silence is a world of comfort.

As we beat over the fields of conversation, we happened upon one we had not talked of for a long time, the world of our youth, from the late 1940s on. We found a number of items common to both. I observed that my three children had grown up in a world almost totally different from that of my youth. And we both acknowledged that the kind of life we lived has all but vanished from the earth, from America anyway, for better and worse.

The ultimate result, four years in the writing, is this little piece of personal history. Perhaps the world does not need another memoir, especially from one who has caused very few ripples in that world. But I think that every piece of life held on to is worth holding on to. Writing is the best amber to preserve it. And I'm a man of leisure. Here 'tis.

Chapter 1

There I Was

In *An American Childhood* Annie Dillard remembers growing up in Pittsburgh in the 1950s. She says that when everything else is gone from her mind and memory she will remember topography, how the land lay, intimately hers in childhood. My home's topography is vivid enough— Piedmont Virginia, specifically Greene County—with its hills and springs and runlets, "branches" to us always; those hills and streams wooded with oak, tulip poplar almost as big as smaller redwood, and several kinds of pine, the astringent smell of a hot summer day in the woods; with undergrowth of chinquapin and wild blueberries, known to Virginians always as huckleberries; and with nearly a third of the horizon overlooked by the aptly named Blue Ridge Mountains, with all of its hollows, from Shifflett to Bacon. The topography is there in my memory, vivid still.

And yet, yet, when all else is gone from my sentient mind, I would guess there would remain as the deepest wayback, the ur-memory of my life, the rhythm of the rural year. Lilacs bloomed in April, when the new-plowed land was full of promise. On the first of May we could shuck our shoes, no matter how chilly the ground or how warm it had been before Mayday. In late August Daddy's watermelons were ripe, heralded by Mama's Aunt Clemmie sending a message: "Tell Raleigh Baugher to let me know when his watermelons are ripe, 'cause I'm coming to visit." And she did, for two glorious weeks, this wonderful 80-plus-year-old woman who kept a twist of tobacco wrapped in the top of her full-length stockings beneath her long dress, which she delicately chewed when she set in to talking, between watermelon feasts. Late September was chinquapin time, our fingers sore from the burrs, the older kids trying to win the younger ones' nuts by playing Oh Horse. And on and on, each year slowly playing out its cycles, each the same as that before and still slightly different with age.

Great-Aunt Clemmie, watermelon gourmand, in her 80s in the 1950s.

i—Waking Up

Unlike my brother Roy, who claimed to remember things that the rest of us calculated must have happened shortly after he exited the womb, I was not a prodigy of memory. Later, my students can vouch, I could remember whole long poems by A. E. Housman and complete exchanges of conversation in a Toni Cade Bambara story, but not daily details before I was four. Perhaps I have a few filmy images before I was four years old, but they are not many, anyway not substantial.

I can remember sleeping in bed with Mama and Daddy, but Mama slept with all of her babies in the crook of her arm all night long, so that she would not roll over on them and could nurse them during the night when they were hungry. I doubt that there was ever a baby bed in the house. Still, being the last of the babies, I stayed in my parents' bed an unusually long time, and when I moved, I moved only to a daybed in that same bedroom, which doubled as a sitting room, especially in winter, when it was one of only two or three rooms with a wood heater. My brothers and sisters—there being four of each—slept two to a double bed, two double beds to a room, in the two unheated bedrooms upstairs in the newer part of the house.

I can remember nursing at my mother's breast, but this is no prodigious feat of memory. Earlier, each new child, on average one every two years, pushed the preceding child to be weaned. As my sister Kay, four years older than I, delighted in telling large mixed company, "Mama like to never weaned Glynn: he sucked titty milk till he was four years old." It's true, as I well remember. Mama, no doubt desperate to get rid of this last hanger-on, with the collusion of my older brothers and sisters there at the time, decided to wean me and smeared her breast with shoe polish. As I went in for a tiny suckle after my solid meal, I pulled back my head, wailing, as my siblings popped up behind Mama, laughing and shaming me. I was weaned.

When I was in the four-to-five age range, Daddy sold the calf of our beautiful Guernsey cow, Cherry (one of usually three milk cows), and we bought an electric washing machine, a Maytag, in my memory still a wonder. The house had been wired for electricity only a short time before, though the Rural Electrification Act of FDR had been reaching out since the 1930s. Pete LeTellier—and I can't tell you how a man with an elegant French name came to be living on a dirt road just over in Albemarle County, just above Scribner's Bridge—wired the house. He put an overhead light in each of the eight rooms and the two halls and one outlet in each of the eight rooms, none in the upstairs or downstairs hall. I remember crawling under the house, which sat up on stacked or single foundation rocks, to watch Pete LeTellier crawl under the house to do the wiring. I did a lot of silent watching in my youth, seeing lots of everything and probably remembering most.

Before the Maytag, Mama did all of the family wash on a ridged glass scrub board sitting in one of two big zinc-plated washtubs. Recently, at an antique store I finally found just such a scrub board, which I have hung in my utility room, close to the Maytag washer and dryer, a tiny memorial to that hard-, hard-, hard-working woman. Even with the electric washing machine, with its leisured oscillation back and forth and its scary rollers that the wise child pushed clothes through with a stick—though a mama disdained to affect such fears—we had to tote bucket after bucket up the hill from the spring to heat over an open fire in a great big short-tripod cast iron kettle sitting on bricks. We did not get water in the house until I was nearly in high school and never had hot water or a bathroom. Some hot water came from the tank on the right end of the wood cookstove, always fired up in winter and fired up for Mama's massive meals for hours even on the hottest summer days. We also heated water in a big cast iron tea kettle and in any vessel available.

All of the older children had to do homework by the feeble light of kerosene lamps. I well remember the lamps, the globes blacked up with soot after one long night's study. In later years, after electrification, Mama always seemed to think of a 40-watt bulb as the zenith of illumination, all that anybody with proper eyesight ever needed. Before the homeplace had the mad, mad luxury of 40-watt lighting and other electrical amenities, my two oldest sisters—Hazel, 17 years older, and Violet, 15 years older—had graduated from high school (with just eleven grades until the 1950s) and left home. I cannot remember their ever living at home. Hazel had wanted to go to Berea College, in Kentucky, a work college that catered to poor and mostly rural counties in Appalachia. But Daddy told her she couldn't, and she never did. (Years later, in enlightened 1960, when Daddy told me I couldn't go to college, I muttered, mostly silently and mostly to myself, "We'll just see.") Gail, Violet's oldest child, said at Violet's funeral in 2013 that her mother wanted to flee the farm so much that she managed to get a beautician's certification in Charlottesville, 20 miles away, and hitchhiked to Baltimore immediately thereafter. For our local area, Baltimore was the cynosure of all eyes, where labor and jobs lay—and some family—though Richmond was much closer and Washington 40 miles closer than Baltimore.

I don't remember our ever having a vehicle to drive. Before my time, Daddy had a little truck. Once, with a bunch of children on back, he accidentally hit the accelerator instead of the brake and ran through the fencing of the chicken lot. Afraid of what might have happened, he was always down on "gas-buggies"—he was born in 1897—spitting out the word so contemptuously when cursing cars that Larry and I always thought he was saying "gas bucket." Daddy was a talented, but not prodigally inventive, cusser all of his life, even after he became a Baptist in his late years. From my earliest days I knew that a lot of people were cock-suckers or son-of-a-bitching "bastuds." That chicken-fence-crashing truck body lay over on the hillside, rusting into elegance, a remnant of a bygone age that Larry and I wondered about long before hearing its provenance. A few photos from 1948 show a short, powerful dually truck with standards for hauling pulpwood, but I don't really remember it. Perhaps Fred, 18 in 1948, drove it. I'm sure that we did not have it long.

So we walked most places. We walked the nearly 2 ½-mile round trip to the local general store to buy a nickel chocolate-coated ice cream bar. We walked the four or five miles one way—Mama and usually June, Kay, Larry, and I—to visit Mama's brother, Christopher Columbus McDaniel—Brother Mac, his wife, Sis (Eleanor), and our favorite first cousins, Mildred, Patricia, and Brenda-too-young-to-be-as-much-fun. It was not unknown for Daddy, ever impatient, to walk 20 miles on a simple fishing trip. The man cured me of fishing for ever after: fish for a while in a choice hole on Chapman's River (Swift Run on maps), find them not biting, jump up and walk five miles to another choice fishing hole; repeat, jump, walk.

The older boys often rode their bicycles places we young ones didn't venture. They spent long summer days adding a link or removing a link from bicycle chains, oiling the chains, tightening the spokes, sanding and rubber-patching inner tubes with match-lit glue and Monkey Grip patches. Fred, Carl, and Roy, but Roy especially, could assemble a bicycle from a scrap heap, I thought, and, his hormones raging, Roy could not be kept from riding to see Laura Ann Courtney, or any other girl except one who yearned for HIM, miles away. Once he returned from such a trip when he was supposed to be "chopping corn"—the local term for getting the weeds out—and Daddy, such was his temper, went after his bicycle with an axe and, let's say, incapacitated it. Didn't matter: Roy had wheels soon again thereafter, though perhaps he paid a bit more attention to the work he was s'posed to be doing on any given day.

ii—The House and Environs

The homeplace was a big old weatherboarded farm house, not unlike dozens of houses in that time, in that place. It still stands and is lived in right now. It had belonged to my father's parents, John Ira Baugher and Cora James [not Jane] Lamb Baugher. I don't know just when they moved there, to Celt, Virginia, seven miles from the seat of Greene County, Stanardsville. The back part of the house, a slightly off-center stem of a T, once had as kitchen what had later been separated and became our meathouse. The old part of the house had two rooms downstairs and two up. The crossbar of the T was added to this in 1918, and this new part of the house also had two largish square rooms downstairs and up, and each floor in the new part had a hall running its length. Every room and the halls in the new part of the house had tongue-and-groove boards for wall and ceiling and 3 or 3 ½-inch flooring, mostly covered with linoleum.

The house was totally uninsulated and sat up on large rocks. It looked fragile but has withstood hurricanes and scores of years. Under the house was a favorite biding place for chickens fluffing up the dusty soil, dogs seeking cool breezes in the summer, and little boys who liked getting dirty. Most places had 15 inches or less of space, but that's plenty for a five-year-old. Until I was 13 or so—old enough to help with the painting—the house was unpainted and naturally weathered like old barns one sees. In an old picture of Grandma and Granddaddy standing beside the house in the 1920s, I guess, the house looks whitewashed; however, I think this is just the sunlight's effect in a black-and-white photo.

The house in 1948, unpainted, sitting on its foundation of stacked rocks. Siblings Carl, 16, with our cat Monroe; Fred, 18, with his dog Rover; and Hazel, 21, standing in the doorway.

Granddaddy Baugher was the postmaster of Celt from 1909 (perhaps when the post office was first opened, when Borneo faded away) to 1934 (when it probably closed), and the one-room building that we still called The Post Office in my youth was a storage outbuilding for tools, chicken mash, and generalized clutter incident to country living. My sister Kay, the seventh child, was always finding around The Post Office Indian-head pennies, buffalo nickels, and occasionally a Liberty dime after hard rains.

The Celt post office of my Granddaddy Baugher in the background of this picture from 1948; also a glimpse of the dually truck used to haul pulpwood; Hazel and her husband, Joe Clayson, both 21.

I never knew Granddaddy Baugher, for he died over four years before I was born, in March 1939. After his death and the loss of his postmaster's pay and his truck-farming selling of produce in Charlottesville, Grandma could no longer carry on and moved to Baltimore to live with her youngest child, Aunt Lucille, and her husband, Odell Sprouse. In the early 1940s, I think in 1942, the homeplace and its attendant 63 acres were to be sold at auction so that the small amount in taxes could be paid. Daddy had been working at the hyperactive Baltimore shipbuilding docks once the War started, making good money, living in the attic at Aunt Lucille's during the War, while Mama and the remaining larger children took care of home. He bought the land and house, I think for about $2,000 (I've seen the deed but am not sure that I remember the date or the price exactly), with his brother-in-law Milton Estes bidding against him; it's possible that Uncle Milton was trying to save the house for Grandma.

Our family—Mama, Daddy, and eight children—had been living at The Old House (you could hear the caps) on Uncle Ernest's place, just across the hill from the homeplace, living in a small house with two rooms downstairs and one large loft-like room upstairs. I was to be the only child of the nine to be born at what became our homestead. Earlier, Mama and Daddy's family had lived for short periods with her parents, with his parents, or in Baltimore in a bungalow; but I gathered all of this information only piecemeal and quite imperfectly.

The house when I came to know it in the late '40s was probably less than it once had been. It may have had a porch or porches in its heyday but none in my youth. The front steps were two large natural rocks. I can remember when the dining room was where it is today and when the rotten floor was taken up, not to be replaced for quite a few years. The dining room and kitchen combined moved to the left front room, previously a parlor. The kitchen floor in the old part of the house was still sound enough to be used as a kitchen in the hot summer, though this entailed a lot of carrying, from one end of the house to the other, so that we could eat summer meals in relative coolness. In the old kitchen sat the glorious Maytag washing machine. In the partly gutted dining room, the floor was trodden earth, and we kept firewood for the cookstove and heaters there year-round.

We ate at a long homemade table, perhaps ten feet by four, which had been our grandparents' before ours. No one visiting the homeplace that knew its history could refrain from mentioning the groaning board, laden with the meals of Grandma Baugher and Mama in turn. Mama said that Grandma, at a huge meal, could tell you how many biscuits each diner ate. Aunt Dolly, Daddy's middle sister, especially delighted in painting the picture of meals of yore. She would stay with us for short periods and take Larry and me blackberrying and wild blueberrying.

The outbuildings were The Post Office, the meathouse, the springhouse, a board-and-batten chicken house, a new and fine big barn, a woodshed (a bit later), and the outhouse. Down the hill below the barn, along the stream that flowed through the springhouse, was the pig pen—not really a building but with some buildingish jury-rigged protection for the porkers.

The meathouse was the only locked building on the place. I never thought about it, but the house was never locked—most of it unlockable—in my childhood. But the hams, shoulders, sidemeat, and other cured meat from our pigs—usually five if I remember correctly—were valuable and not to be trusted to the goodness of people. I doubt that anyone would have stolen it, but better safe. It had one window, but that was shuttered inside. Inside, the springy floor was always more than a little bit greasy and salt-spattered. The meat was kept in a deep, heavy wooden box and was coated in lots of salt, black pepper, and sometimes brown sugar cure. I remember the big dark blue Morton tins, I think a mixture of brown sugar and salt, used in some of the curing. We had no smoke house and never improvised. I don't think we cared especially for smoked meat. We never had beef. Strangely enough, some old shoe lasts and other outmoded tools like a froe and an adze were kept in the meathouse. Of course, they were a rusted mess from all of the salt. But Daddy was never the best organized or the most efficient of men. Uncle Ernest had all of his tools hung, each in its own special place in the backroom of his slightly more primitive house.

Most of the meathouse is visible, also a sawbuck and the back corner of the old part of the house; sister Kay, nearly 9.

Downhill perhaps a hundred yards from the house was the springhouse. Built of wood, both in its shell and the springbox, it tended to decay, but it was newish when I was a small boy and served wonderfully well all the purposes of refrigeration before we got a refrigerator, when I was perhaps 11 or 12; even then the springhouse served to hold excess milk that, when skimmed of cream for making butter, was allowed to clabber so we could make cottage cheese. The spring was our sole source of water, cold in even the hottest weather, flowing from deep down in the rocks. No water has ever tasted as good to me since, especially from the most moss-laden rock holes. In very hot weather it might get a bit of algae in the slowest parts, which we, in our witty country ways, called "frog shit," but it still tasted good. About twenty feet below the spring was the springhouse, its most important part being a box that ran the length of the small building, through which the spring overflow ran. Plunged in this were crocks of milk and cream, butter floating in a jar in summertime, with cucumbers and melons in season keeping cool. Before each meal, we went to the springhouse to retrieve milk, drunk at every meal. After each milking, the buckets were taken to the springhouse, along with warm, soapy water for washing up after the milk was strained. When I was a teenager, I helped Mama milk the three cows and did all of the springhouse work for a while.

The barn, built in fine fashion by Mama's younger brother, Uncle Jinks the carpenter, replaced a ramshackle old barn that I can barely remember. To the right of the nicely timbered central hall were the mangers and three milking stalls. The head cow, Bossy, the fine Jersey cow in my youth, would go in first and stop in the first stall. The other two cows would have to squeeze in behind her to go to the second and third stalls. Out of an old chest icebox in the middle of the barn each cow got a scoop of molasses-fragrant dairy feed to make them eager to be milked. I liked to watch the cows lick their slick, drooling tongues up over their noses and into their nostrils to get all of the manna snuffed up. Following the European fashion, it was milkmaids when milkmaids were available. When no one was left at home but Larry and me, we were drafted, but Larry never made a go of it: his fingernails he always kept long, insisting that it hurt to cut fingernails, and he was a bit inept at things like milking. Mama used to milk two cows most of the time to my one, but I got rather proficient. However, I lacked her skill in hitting the cats' mouths with streams of warm milk.

Mama's two brothers as young men, Uncle Jinks on the left, the
carpenter who built our barn, and "Brother Mac," Christopher
Columbus McDaniel, the father of Mildred, Patricia, and Brenda.

On the left of the central hall of the barn was a stall sometimes used
to feed calves from a teated bucket, supplement or, rarely, a necessity. Here,
later, Larry kept his lone pig, Wilbur, named not so much for the pig in
Charlotte's Web as for the Greene County sheriff, Wilbur "Hooks" Deane,
when Larry had to do a Vo-Ag project in high school, taking that course
as a lesser evil than algebra. In the enclosed section on the left side of
the barn, Daddy stacked, sorted, rubbed clean, and reshifted his beloved
potato crop. I don't believe that Paddy the stereotypical Irishman loved
potatoes so well as Daddy. He ate them every day and always grew about
50 bushels of them each year. He would feed the smallest ones to the pigs
only when Mama rebelled at trying to peel them.

The upstairs of the barn, one large, high open room, was for fodder
and hay for the cows in winter. It always smelled good, as a proper barn
should, but it was dusty to hide in, dusty for the first tentative solo sexual

exploration of an unnamed subteen boy. When we were younger, we delighted in jumping the eight or nine feet out of the barn loft, barefooted, to the ground. No bones were ever broken, for fate is often kind to the stupid.

Whereas the two biggest buildings on the place, our house and the barn, were weatherboarded—overlapped long horizontal boards to keep the weather out, also called clapboarding—the chicken house and, later, the woodhouse were of board-and-batten construction, vertical boards with narrow strips nailed over the joints. One can see why: the chickens and firewood were to be protected from wind-driven rain and other "falling weather," as snow, hail, and other inclemencies were called.

The chickens were a valued part of our overall "oeconomy," as it used to be called in older times than mine. They were nearly always free range, running around pecking at bits of food or more-than-ordinarily-interesting little bits of nastiness they could find. When they got broody, they would find all sorts of out-of-the way places to lay their eggs. The children had the job of trying to find the hens' nests before they set in to incubating the eggs. If baby chicks were wanted, we wanted them to be hatched in the nests in the chicken house. We had probably twenty-four nest boxes, in three rows, mostly well-filled with hay. A broody hen, trying to build up a nest of eggs, was ill-tempered and would peck anyone trying to get eggs from under her. In springtime and summer, we nearly always had at least one set of baby chicks, their mothers scratching in the dirt, singing, and chuk-chukking to the chicks, as roosters sometimes did for their hens.

We ordinarily had about twenty-five to thirty hens, with but one rooster, usually, to serve them. We never called them cocks, knowing that that was indecent language. Occasionally a rooster grew mean and tried to spur people. If he was not the only rooster, Mama did not hesitate in destining him for the stewpot. The eggs we ate, then, were doubtlessly fertile eggs, if that made any difference.

Our own chickens were eaten on special occasions, usually young ones. Anyone who has ever seen a chicken with its head cut off with a hatchet or axe will always remember the flopping around in the dust, life surrendering only slowly. In a pinch, Mama could steel herself to the job, but it was usually done by Daddy or my older brothers, all unflinching. I certainly never did it, though I ate the chickens with gusto.

Occasionally the chickens got too rambunctious in their food-foraging and would scratch in Daddy's beloved potato patches. Then their wings would be clipped, and they would be confined to the chicken lot. My older siblings can remember Daddy's jow-rowing (Mama's word) on and on about the chickens. I think Mama sold them all once, tired of listening to the man, until the absence of eggs was felt so badly that the flock was restarted. In the springtime the rural mailman's car nearly always had boxes of baby chicks peeping away on the back seat, gotten through mail-order.

Though our "cash-flow" was very small, sometimes non-existent when I was a small boy, we usually found money enough—Daddy would cut a few loads of pulpwood, perhaps—to buy laying mash for the chickens when they couldn't get enough food naturally. I often fed the chickens and fumed that the birdbrains could not find a gate opening but tried to go straight through the chicken wire to get at the laying mash. Taking everything irrational as a private insult, I wailed, "Stupid chickens! Why did God make chickens so dumb?" My mother responded, "How smart do you have to be just to get your head chopped off?" My mother the philosopher.

On rare occasions a hawk zoomed down, seized in its talons, and carried off a young chicken, causing Mama great worry and distress. Here was part of our life support being ripped away. Daddy would sit on guard with his shotgun, and the threat passed. On rarer occasions a fox would carry off a chicken, always putting the whole of that little world in an uproar. You haven't heard screeching until you've heard a flock of upset chickens.

The eggs—we got at least a dozen a day nearly always and usually far more—were kept in a basket, unrefrigerated, in the European fashion. We ate them always for breakfast, and Mama used them for baking cakes and puddings. I've never been able to duplicate her delicious egg-and-cream-rich baked rice pudding, and I suspect that it must have had more eggs than I've ever ventured. Leghorns, Rhode Island Reds, and, in the early days, barred black-and-white Dominechers were our main chickens—good 'uns all. Occasionally Roy experimented with keeping bantams, always called banties, but I think that was mostly a money-making scheme. The eggs were too little to be of much use.

One would think that the last building on the place—the outhouse, outdoor john, or toilet—would have profited from being board-and batten construction, for privacy. But it never had battens, just vertical boards. I didn't feel overly sensitive about having no indoor bathroom, mostly because almost none of our neighbors did either. We dug a hole about six feet deep and nearly the same in length and breadth and built a little shed over it. Sometimes a little lime was sprinkled down after use, but not usually. In later years we sometimes had a store-bought toilet seat and toilet paper, but in my youth it was mainly just a well-carved hole in a wide board for seat and old Sears or Montgomery Ward catalogs or newspapers for toilet paper. Overly delicate youth were always corrected with the reprimand, "Oh, don't be so nasty-nice." I was gratified, years later, to discover that one of the early meanings of "nice" was "overly fastidious." When boys, at least, were out playing and had to pee, there were thousands of trees to step behind and probably no one around within at least a quarter mile, so that was that.

Chapter 2

One-Room Schooling

When I was nearly five years old and all of my brothers and sisters still at home were in school in early September, the rhythm of the year meant something brand-new and not very welcome: I was the only child around the house for long-houred days, long especially in winter. Oh, I profited by the distinction, for I hung around with Mama most of the time, watching her cook. I learned things that I didn't know I was learning at the time—the natural, improvised ways of cooking with whatever was to hand.

My brothers and sisters—June, Kay, and Larry especially— were eager to teach me whatever they learned in school. Of course I learned to read, print, and do simple arithmetic long before starting school, if months and months can be called "long." In fair weather I would sit on the group of mailboxes down by the road—ours, Uncle Ernest's, and Fannie Early's— and watch the children at play up at Celt Elementary School, across the dirt road and a bit over a hundred yards up the hill. I heard new words that I didn't know, such as "library," which got criss-crossed in my head with "lilac" so that I wasn't quite sure what it was.

Celt was not big enough even to call a hamlet. It never consisted of more than the post office that my grandfather ran, my grandparents' house, and the elementary school. In a larger sense, to include all of the children that went to Celt School, it might have been considered to go to the Albemarle County line, less than a mile "down" the road from our home. Going south on that dirt road, 604, toward Charlottesville was always considered going down the road. Going north, toward Stanardsville, was going "up" the road. In this direction, Celt may have been considered to extend about two miles, to Amicus, though Amicus was nothing but a little polling place and a Seventh-Day Adventist Church. But it sat at a crossroads—to the right were Quinque and Ruckersville; to the left were Dyke and Geer; straight ahead was Stanardsville, the county seat. Celt School also drew students from a couple of miles up a side road, about a half mile up the road from our home. This was called the New Road, and the school district ended once again at the Albemarle County line.

That classical names peppered the landscape probably says something about the education of people doing the naming. "Amicus" means "friend." About three or four miles from Amicus lay Quinque, Latin for "five," probably so named because it was the fifth post stop on the road, or so Laura C. Moyers, who taught Latin at the high school in Stanardsville, said. "Celt," always pronounced with an –s sound, never a –k sound, was doubtlessly found in Caesar's commentaries on his wars with the Celts. Daddy told me once that he remembered a few Latin words from school, including *agricola* (farmer), and remembered the story of Daedalus and Icarus and the lament "Alas, poor Icarus" (He pronounced it EYE.ca.rus) when the wax wings of the son melted as he soared up too close to the sun. So Latin was common in the instruction even at lower levels.

No matter how small, rural hamlets and smaller settlements needed their own school, post office, and polling place. Early in the twentieth century few rural people had cars, and though a walk of four or five miles might be required, reaching these necessities on foot was not deemed a special hardship. My mother and her older sister, Bonnie, for a time walked that distance to go to school at Celt, until Mama fell off a swinging bridge and almost drowned, her sister pulling her from the water.

Celt Elementary School was altogether on a more ambitious plan than the little cubicle of a polling place and the little post office. The front steps of the school house were concrete, though the foundation of the building was only a series of big rocks, like our house, on which the sills of the building were set. Though only one room was used for classes when Kay, Larry, and I were there, more of the building had been used earlier, and there had been more than the five grades that were there in the 1950s. Some of our older brothers and sisters had gone there when both of the two large downstairs rooms were used, when there were seven grades at the school.

Celt Elementary School as it was in the 1930s, left half and center.
The family is not mine. I remember the belfry as being different,
but perhaps not. Thanks to Geneva Morris Shifflett.

I don't know when the school was built. I think that Daddy, born in 1897, went to school there, but I'm not sure whether the building was the same. Public school systems were not officially established in Virginia until 1870. In 1906 Greene County had eleven white schools. Celt was doubtlessly one of them.

Though I can remember what eons the calendar for 1948 contained, and what ages the first eight months of 1949, in early September of 1949, one month shy of my sixth birthday, I finally got to go to school. It had evoked all sorts of speculations and longings when I watched the children at recess time. Now I was there. Though Larry, ever the social isolate, was never particularly thrilled with school, I loved it from the first day. Miss

Towne, our teacher, was the stereotyped schoolmarm of earlier days, a spinster, two years younger than Mama (then 41), a thin, angular woman with prominent and sharp hazel eyes, a North Carolinian orphan or deserted child with only a sister in the world, Mama's friend Inez, also unmarried, living in Cincinnati, a kind of governess.

Miss Mary Katherine Towne, usually called Kay by those who knew her well.

Miss Towne lived with two elderly women—a widow, Mrs. Fannie Davis Early, and her sister-in-law, Miss Sally-Betty Early—in a huge and once-genteel but now rather ramshackle house from pre-Civil War days a half-mile or so down in the hollow on what was once a big farm with slaves. We heard stories of Union soldiers riding into the house. The Earlys had been moderately big in the Confederacy. Miss Sally-Betty was very hard of hearing, a little dotty, and the household altogether strange to the view of us kids. Miss Towne had a Great Dane dog named Diana, which we rather feared, but we liked visiting. They had a piano, on which June and Kay played "Punch the Devil's Eyeballs Out," a classic, and a large stock of books on shelves up a narrow, twisting staircase, cloth carpets, and a room that once must have seen large dancing-parties, fording the river from the direction of Albemarle County. The room had a painted mural, I think of a ballroom scene, on the walls. The whole house could have been dropped down into Faulkner country with no questions asked.

From this hole Miss Mary Katherine (Kay) Towne walked to school on fine days and drove at other times. I don't remember having much snow while we were at Celt Elementary School, but the road was often a morass of mud, and a little stream ran across it in two places near the house down in the hollow. Miss Towne drove a dark green, boxy Chevrolet made in the 1930s and called it Mr. Green until sometime in the early 1950s she bought a brand-new gray Ford, which she dubbed Mrs. Gray. We used to go out on the school lot and make faces into the shiny bumpers, laughing at our makeshift hall-of-mirrors.

When we younger children were in Celt School in the late 1940s and early 1950s, only one room was being used, on the left side of the building. The room was perhaps 25 or 30 feet square, or nearly square, with a high, high ceiling. On the back wall of the room a blackboard ran nearly all the way across. The room was badly heated by a tin wood heater close to the middle of the room with a high right-angled tin stovepipe supported by wires from the ceiling. The flue was apparently just beyond the wall, in the cloak closet. The school had no electricity or water but had a wellhouse and iron pump for water outside and two outdoor toilets, one for boys, one for girls and Miss Towne.

The classroom had large windows facing more or less south and east, with canvas cloth blinds to raise or lower when the sun was too intense. The windows had wooden wells at the bottom, forming a triangular trough when viewed from the ends, so that fresh air could come in without there being a direct draft. Galvanized strong wire screens woven in rectangles like garden fencing covered the outside of the windows.

Twenty-plus students made up the five grades, the first- and second-graders in small woven-bottom chairs surrounding brown-painted oak tables with six or eight openings between the tabletop and the underside of the table. These cubbies held our books, papers, pencils, crayons, and other needments. The third, fourth, and fifth graders sat in rows of double-seated desks with legs of cast iron, seats of smooth, curved wood, and desk tops that were attached to the back of the seat in front. The tops of the desks had holes for inkwells still. We usually had a double desk to ourselves, for rarely were there more than five people to a grade. These three rows of desks all faced the blackboard at the back of the room.

In the front right corner (as viewed from outside), near the door to the entrance hall, sat the teacher's desk with a wooden shelf on the wall holding a globe and a small row of harder books, including a big dictionary. Our library was contained mainly in a vivid red wooden cabinet, about the size of a medium bookcase, standing against the right-hand wall. The books were fairly usual for the time: I remember a stack of Bobbsey Twins books, one on Kit Carson, one on the Dionne quints, and so on.

In the front left corner was our "sand table," as it was always called, though it was a large wooden table with raised sides on it containing not sand but sawdust. On this we built scenes, mostly for geography, using egg shells for igloos and cotton for snow in an Eskimo landscape, wooden sticks for log cabins, panes of glass with blue paper under them for ocean, sometimes palm trees and the natural sawdust for the desert. Quite often our attempts were futile, like the prairie sod house we tried to build by leaning hunks of sod (cut with a butcher knife) against a twig frame. I'm not sure that our teacher knew that sod houses were made of sod used like brick.

In the back left corner of the room the teacher displayed the best papers from the beginning students and had the star board, where we got gold, silver, or colored stars, quite proudly, for excellence, mostly in reading. Above the blackboard hung some roll-down maps and, running across, the cursive alphabet, upper and lower case. Sometimes, above this, pictures from special projects, such as the fifth grade's study of manufactory, were displayed. I remember especially the ranks of shoes to illustrate that Massachusetts was shoe-manufacturer to the country.

On the right-hand wall under the stovepipe arch, art work was sometimes displayed. I remember getting a Puss-in-Boots (ever the cat-lover) hung there in a crude wooden frame that I made from the end of an orange crate. Toward the back of this wall, near the second-grade table, a door opened into a large closet or cloak room, where we hung our coats and stowed our galoshes and caps. This room had a window that was loose-screened and unlocked, through which we Baugher children boosted each other to snoop around the school during closed hours, mostly in the summer. The front door was kept locked, but Mama had an extra key to it, and we often went in that way, with a thrill of danger at the prospect that Miss Towne might drive up to the school or by the school for something when we were inside.

Entering the large front door, the school's only outside door, one stood in an entry hall, directly facing the door to the staircase. To the left was our classroom and the closet, the top of which was visible to the left of the banister as one went upstairs. To the right of the staircase, symmetrically matching the closet on the left, was a small room used for storage. On the right end of the building was an exact duplicate of the left classroom, reversed, except that it had no desks then. It had some work tables, piles of slab wood during the cold months, a good deal of junky stuff left over from the time that home economics was taught there. The most eye-catching item was a big wooden box sitting in the front corner. I don't know what the box was for. It looks in my memory's eye like a box for storing salted meat, as we had out in our meathouse, but the older children told the first-graders that a dead woman was kept in the box. I don't know about the others, but I certainly believed the story and was quite afraid of the box and the room at first.

At the top of the staircase was a landing with a step or two going off to either side. But there was no room division upstairs, just one large room, though the left side had a stage raised about a foot above the general floor level. Clearly this was an auditorium, meant to be used for stage presentations, from a more ambitious time. We never used the upstairs at all. It was quite dusty and cluttered with old desk pieces, folding wooden chairs, a big boiler/canner tub, and various junk. We were rarely allowed to go upstairs. It seemed to be considered unsafe. Perhaps we sneaked through the doors that closed in the staircase when we did get to go up there. Of course we visited the upstairs when we sneaked into the empty building, but it was always a bit derelict and creepy.

The caretaking of the building was left to the teacher, who got there early on cold mornings and started the fire. We usually gathered around the stove before classes began, while the room warmed up, especially when frost crystals stood up on top of the red-mud banks at the side of the deep-rutted road that ran back in the hollow to the old Early place. I pitied the poor girls who shivered in their dresses. No girl wore pants to school then, and poor, slight Allie Shifflett looked almost blue or transparent from the cold.

In addition to building fires, Miss Towne took care of the floors, which were oiled to keep down dust, and probably swabbed the toilet seats occasionally, for I remember seeing Lysol bottles in the outdoor toilets. The girls' toilet was to the left behind the school building. To the right, symmetrically placed, was the boys'. Each was a two-seater, I think, and had a right-angled high wooden fence attached to the toilet, shielding the door from view.

Near the left front corner of the building was a little windowless wellhouse with a green iron pump that small children could just manage, jumping up and down for a good counting time until the water started to flow. We each had a drinking cup or collapsible tumbler on a shelf. The water had a distinct iron taste, not the good taste of our spring water.

We Baughers went home for lunch, but those who commuted (some on foot, some on the bus that went on to the high school in Stanardsville) were expected to bring their lunch and washed their hands with a sliver of soap and the cold water that trickled from the bottom of a cracked zinc bucket. In earlier years hot lunches had been cooked at the school, when the population was greater and things run on a bigger scale. Miss Towne brought what we thought of as exotic lunches, always including store-bought fruit, but the poorer children sometimes had what revolted me, cold fried-egg sandwiches. We had good full hot lunches (dinners actually, for our big meal was in the middle of the day) at home. Going by an old arched rectangular clock kept on the kitchen pie-safe, Mama almost always had the meal ready on time, though the biscuits were sometimes still in the oven, coming out just in time to be put aswim in butter.

At school after lunch and after all play periods we lined up in front of the steps leading up to a small porch before trooping into the building. Miss Towne rang a small bronze handbell part of the time. At other times students were allowed to swing the rope of the big bell hung in the belfry tower on top of the building. We got into line, first grade to fifth, with the fifth-grade boys always jostling to see who could be the last in line to go in.

The outside of the building was a peeling whitish weatherboarding, I think the white being whitewash rather than any kind of paint, but the general impression was weathered gray-white. Some pains had been taken to make the school a bit homey. A lilac bush grew at the left front corner and another near the wellhouse. A peach tree, a thick scattering of daffodils, and at least one yucca plant grew near the wellhouse. But the playground was whatever we could make of it. Around the building the ground was worn rather bare from lots of running. In the small space between the back of the school and the fence that separated it from the Early woods we played Giant Step, Red Rover, and other such baseline games.

Huge oak trees stood behind the school and ran at intervals down to the road on the right side of the building. In among a half dozen trees, near the boys' toilet, was the only tolerably flat place for Mush-pot, a highly favored game, a baseline game that involved capturing the opposing team's "men" and putting them in jail one at a time. We also played squat-tag there, and sometimes our smaller town-ball games. But the fence and trees made it less than ideal for those. Town-ball was played with a tennis or soft-rubber ball, similar to the game of softball, with the chief differences being that catching the ball on the first bounce was an out and that you could get a base-runner out not just by tagging him/her but by throwing the ball at the runner and hitting him/her. All games at the two recess periods were full-school games and included all of the boys and the girls. Some of our stronger players delighted in hitting the base-runner as hard as possible, but their eagerness to hurt made their throws often inaccurate. We usually moved downhill a bit for town-ball games, though the field was uneven and there was a clump of sycamore right in the way toward second base. First base ran downhill, and it was a bit uphill to third. Our bats were usually flat planks hacked narrow at the handle. Of course, there was no athletic equipment budget for the school, just what we could make or come up with.

Before classes in the morning, at lunchtime, and as students waited for the bus at the end of the day, play was more disorganized. Though girls sometimes played hopscotch or jumped rope and boys rarely, in the time before classes began or at lunchtime, our games for the standard recess periods, morning and afternoon, were chosen by democratic vote. We voted in line at the door, next to the pencil sharpener, before going out. We got in line for everything, to teach us orderliness. The games were usually unsupervised but ran according to the rules. The rules were taught in hand-me-down fashion, and no one ever expected to have grown-ups instruct or intrude in our games. The teacher stayed inside during recess and marked papers. She was outside with us at day's end, and occasionally at other times.

Certain games would go through periods of popularity for days on end and then inexplicably change and not be played for a time. In addition to Mush-pot and town-ball, our favorite was hide and seek, which we called hidin' seek. And the one who was "It" we called "Hit"—"You're Hit." I was gratified years later to realize that it was a hand-me-down English Cockney pronunciation, thrusting an H in where there was none.

Our base for hiding was usually one of the two big white oak trees near the road down to the Early home. We often ran across the gulley-like road and hid in the bushes on the bank.

We had other games that we played fairly often, usually some hell-for-leather running games—Squirrel in a Hollow Tree, Foxes and Hounds, Drop the Handkerchief, Freeze Tag, simple races. It was good to realize later that some of the games were very old traditional English folk games. Some games were more seasonal. When the oak leaves fell in the autumn, we played Dead Man, Dead Man, Rise, burying the one who was "it" under leaves and yelling at him/her to rise and catch us. We sometimes built tall circular houses out of slab wood piled outside. In early fall and after May 1 we usually went to school barefoot, pitying the few students whose mothers would not let them go without shoes. In late May we would arrange a game that would take us to the lower part of the school grounds, near the dirt road so that we could pick wild strawberries.

In warm weather girls often jumped rope, doing hot pepper jumps. Kay was good at this (though, four years older, she was there at the school only one year when I was). The song went, "Mabel, Mabel, set the table. Don't forget the salt and pepper." With the word "pepper" the rope-turners would speed up intensely. They also did high-water turns, accompanied, as were many of our games, by recited rhymes. The boys liked playing high-jump with the ropes stretched taut. In very cold weather we sometimes had ice at the shady right end of the building to slide on. We never played anything like football, but dodgeball, which involves hitting other people with a ball, played with a soccer ball from somewhere, was a favorite.

Indoors, where on very rare occasions we stayed during foul weather, our games were more likely to be "activities." Every Friday afternoon we looked forward to "activity period" when we did a great deal of coloring, cutting out, pasting, and making things. The lower grades made pinwheels to be stuck into the eraser at pencil's end, or walking Dutch girls with rotating legs attached with a paper clasp, paper lanterns, and so on. The higher grades worked at the sand table sometimes. We had a big box of crayons as communal property—huge chunks of color. Some students brought their own boxes of Crayolas or, if the mother had been so foolish as to economize, Blendwel crayons, which we judged to be junk. Sometimes we were allowed to play cards, but this was usually done in otherwise free time. We had reading-aloud period. Sometimes very good fifth-grade readers would get to read to the rest of the school. Once when I got to read my voice shook with nervousness at filling in for Miss Towne. We read fine fairy tales from a big, big story book that may have belonged to Miss Towne.

Sometimes we would get huge packages of things from some agency or other that must have ministered to backwoodsy have-not schools. We got a large number of comic books with "Little Moron" jokes. Sample: Why did the Little Moron throw the clock out of the window? He wanted to see time fly. No political correctness there. I remember Miss Towne telling Mama once that a neighbor boy was a "high-grade moron." Probably once a year there was a clothing box. We took very little of that since we didn't consider ourselves the poor, but occasionally there was something like a coonskin hat (in the Davy Crockett period) that we just had to have. Larry and I sneaked in and got (stole) that hat before the official distribution time because we knew we didn't stand a chance against some of the mountain-hoogies.

Parenthetically, a mountain hoogie (soft G—HOO.jee) or a mountain tacky—used interchangeably— was rougher than the ordinary country poor, usually from the hollows right up in the mountains. A mountain hoogie ate cornbread with gravy, frequently for breakfast, and wore white shirts with bib overalls for Saturday-night outings. Blithely dismissing someone as a mountain tacky gave us a sense of superiority.

The school also got boxes of fresh and dried fruit (government surplus?), such as apricots, from time to time, and everybody shared that equally.

A big event each month was the visit of the Bible-school teacher. One of them, Mrs. Johnson, had an interesting hairnet and a gold tooth. Nobody seemed to mind that the state and religion were being mingled. The adults were not self-conscious, and we weren't embarrassed, as we often were by religion. The teacher had a folding easel with felt figures to illustrate a Bible story, usually one of the better Old Testament stories such as David and Goliath or Joseph's being sold into Egypt. She taught us songs about things like the foolish man who built his house on sand. Birthday people for the month got pretty little bookmarks with a picture and Bible verses. Some of the mountain-tacky families seemed to have birthdays every month. But the teacher would usually go ahead and give the bookmarks to the little liars.

The 4-H Club, an offshoot of the County Agricultural Extension Service, also came each month, in the person of a man to teach the older boys and a woman to teach the girls. The girls were taught some homemaking things, I think, by the wonderfully named Miss Violet Navy. I don't remember learning anything myself from Bogardus Worth, but didn't he have a splendid name to roll over the tongue? I remember Miss Navy's taking us on a picnic on the stream up toward Dyke. For me, it involved Cherry Smash soda pop, the most soul-satisfying soft drink I can recall. Miss Navy asked us all whether we pronounced the capital of Kentucky LOO.is.ville or Looey.ville. We gave our answers, upon which she pertly said, "I pronounce it 'FRANK.fort.'" Yuk-yuk.

All holidays were properly observed with lots of attention to getting the classroom decorated with drawings and cutouts. Christmas always involved learning a program, reciting "The Night Before Christmas" in a series of parts, learning songs, and memorizing short sayings. The fifth-grade boys got to go out all of one morning to cut the best Christmas tree to be found. Mama nearly always came to the Christmas programs, the only guest I remember. We had no music or musical instrument in the school but did a great deal of singing always. "Silent Night" challenged our harmonies: we weren't soft enough. But "Jingle Bells" spoke to our primal energies, and the "Whee, we got upsot" part was fun. Some of the mountain-hoogie girls could sing some robust Holy Roller (Pentecostal) hymns. I remember especially "Roll the Old Chariot Up the Hill," which I am sure the girl sang as "Roll the Old Cherry Up the Hill." The girls often sang at lunchtime; I remember especially "My Bonnie Lies Over the Ocean." We memorized a lot of verse, usually something with a rollicking rhythm like Edward Lear's "The Owl and the Pussycat," and we were all the better for the memory work.

Miss Towne was not a martinet but a strict disciplinarian. A ruler on the outstretched palm, a certain number of licks, was the usual punishment, but out-and-out paddling of the bottom was not unheard of. She had a rather hard time with the obstinate Baugher children. She told Kay that she had a streak of Baugher stubbornness a yard wide down her back. Larry used to crawl under the table and kick Miss Towne on the shins or put his head down on the table and scoot around, away from her. She kept me once after school because I was accused of throwing rocks—an outright lie as I saw it. I refused to hold hands with a girl we called Buzzard, for one of our ring games, and was kept in. I don't recall any parent's questioning Miss Towne's ordinary discipline.

Miss Towne also had troubles with Original Sin rearing its ugly head. Some of the mountain-tacky girls wanted to wear lipstick and other makeup, which we knew was a sin for a grade-school kid, but she made them wash it off and never even bring it to school again. One boy used to delight in unzipping his pants and displaying himself under the table to make the little girls giggle, and Virginia Conley snort. Some really mean boys would occasionally scratch offensive pictures on the outside walls.

She had to teach us everything, from health to etiquette, as she saw it. Every Monday morning we were asked if we had bathed over the weekend. We washed every day, of course, at least what showed, but in the winter we certainly didn't immerse ourselves in a tub of water. (**SHE** had a bathtub and hot water indoors.) Taking a bath to us meant in a tub, but we always lied and raised our hands for having taken a bath, judging that the lie was justified by her butt-inskyness. So did everybody else raise hands, although almost nobody had had her kind of bath. Some kids you could smell, the Great Unwashed. Mrs. Early always said that we Baugher kids were always clean, making a distinction between "clean dirt" and "dirty dirt." We also had health campaigns to encourage things like teeth-brushing. I remember Glenda Lawson's impressive winning poster—"Don't Have Slop-Bucket Teeth"—complete with drawing of a scummy slop-bucket.

How Miss Towne kept five grades going at once is hard to imagine, but school usually worked smoothly. She listened to every first grader read aloud; then one student would walk around the table to tell hard words to students as they read silently while Miss Towne was with another class. I often got to do this, the weight of learning and responsibility sitting heavy on my shoulders. One class might be working at the blackboard, another doing math problems from a book, another working on a geography project at the sand table. A good deal of learning took place at the board. I remember that we did board time every day in the lower grades, learning math problems, spelling, and the cursive alphabet. We also did a lot of reading out loud, reciting, and taking dictation, a favorite French method of teaching composition. The room, you would think, would be a disconcerting babble, but we could often learn from higher grades. I remember knowing how to do all of the fifth-grade math while in the fourth grade. I watched them at the board after quickly finishing my work. And higher grades helped lower ones, such as in "telling words" to first-graders.

The system was flexible: after a month in the second grade—to get me past the age of 6—I was moved to the third grade and thereafter was with Larry through school, one of four people in my class, with Kenny Marshall and Vernell Morris the only other two. And yet I never had a harder grader than Miss Towne. The only C I ever got in any grade report she gave me. She excused us from exams if we had all A's and B's on our report cards, but we had exams, as grade-school children do not today. When I discovered lots of old report cards at home, I was startled to see that both Roy and Fred, both slackers in later grades, apparently bested me in elementary school.

We had no kindergarten, and so most of us learned to read with the primer book, a thin red book about Billy and Jane and their pet monkey, Winky, that got into mischief such as eating crayons at school. The ordinary readers were dull affairs, repeating words in a deranged fashion: "Oh, oh, oh, see Billy. See Billy run. Oh, see Jane run." In a year or two there was a third child, at first called only Baby, his name later revealed to be David.

Our lessons put a great deal of emphasis on spelling, reading, grammar, and handwriting. We were expected to submit entries for the art and handwriting exhibits in the county fair each year. We had good old standby selections in our readers—stories that I remember still, about trolls and goats, patriotic stories about Pocahontas or Lewis and Clark; semi-folk songs like "Home, Home on the Range"; lots of poems by the likes of the Virginian Nancy Byrd Turner, Edward Lear, and A. E. Housman. I still almost remember "When Goody O'Grumpity baked a cake/ The tall reeds danced by the mournful lake." Later, I discovered that this poem was by the Newbery medalist Carol Ryrie Brink. We went heavy on geography, meeting in books representative Eskimos (no Inuits then) or South Sea islanders; and on Virginia history and American history. It still surprises me to find college students ignorant of basic geography lessons or spelling and usage that I learned while in grade school at Celt.

Clearly, we could get the basics at the school. We had none of the courses like music, we weren't graded on our play or art, and Miss Towne did not dispense praise very lightly. Self-esteem was hard-won. We never got trophies. I cannot remember that she ever showed any special affection for children, but she must have had a good deal of dedication.

Looking backward, I rather relish the memory of Celt School. I suppose most of my family felt similarly. There were ugly moments, such as the ones caused by the big and bullying mountain-hoogies, but most of them were gone when Larry and I were there. There were fist fights, including one in which I got a wart knocked off my hand. Shameless teasing and tormenting went on out on the playground. We called people Snaggle-Tooth and Buzzard, and my father was called Sir Walter Raleigh, which we took as a great insult because it was meant to be. With parents named Raleigh and Olga, you have to expect a certain amount of attention, but the children on the whole could not make much of Olga. More often than bad things I remember my winning friend Awood Raines, son of the drunk that tenant-farmed on Mrs. Early's place. Awood glowed with delight at every simple pleasure, red in the face from running, running, running. Then he'd say, "Let's do it a.GEN."

I'm sure that there was a rather pinched-in poverty, but everybody was poor; country poverty is not like city poverty; and it certainly didn't bother me. My first memories are always of the rip-snorting games, the pleasantly chalk-dusty and oily smell of the room, making things to carry home, Easter egg hunts—the vivid sense of place. As young children, we Baughers had watched the children at play, sitting on our front steps, on the mailboxes, in the plum tree down near the road, wanting to go to school up on the hill long before we could start. I was pining away during the school year until I could get up there with Larry and find out what those kids did when I heard them chanting their play-songs and screaming as they ran.

After Larry and I moved on to William Monroe, in Stanardsville, in the sixth grade, Celt School was closed, as part of the county-wide consolidation of local schools. Mama and Daddy had both gone to school some there, and all nine of us Baugher children had gone there, most of us taught by Miss Towne. Not many years afterwards, not long after moving with Miss Sally-Betty to a new house out of the back hollow, Fannie Early now dead, after moving into the sixties with a Volkswagen Beetle to commute to Stanardsville every day, Miss Towne died of cancer. I wish someone had interviewed her to get some more accurate factual materials of how things were taught, to buttress up the fragility of memory.

Miss Towne, Miss Sally-Betty, Fannie ("Pan") Davis Early, and the rest of the Early family lie in the graveyard at what was once Mt. Paran Methodist Church, now a handsome private home converted by an architect. Not far from Miss Towne is the grave of my grandfather, John Ira Baugher, the postmaster, forever apart from Grandma Baugher, buried in the Essex section of Baltimore. Beside Granddaddy Baugher lies my brother Carl, buried in the spring of 2014.

Chapter 3

Eatin's

When Mama called us to meals, she was just about as likely to call "Eatin's ready" as to name the specific meal. I liked, and like, that older English way of designating but not being too specific. Our three meals were breakfast—hearty and big, usually the only meal at which we had meat; dinner (never lunch), which, as the name implies, was our biggest meal of the day; and supper, mostly leftovers from dinner, often eaten at room temperature, never refrigerated even after we got a refrigerator, with hot cornbread and sometimes hot corn muffins, and perhaps added to the fare would be a skillet of newly fried potatoes with onions. Occasionally we would have fried fish, newly caught, for supper, but they were just as likely to fill out the breakfast the next morning. In winter time, when we could catch no fish, we sometimes had fried fish cakes, of salmon or mackerel. Three times a day Mama made from scratch at least one kind of bread. We always had at least biscuits for breakfast and dinner and at least one kind of cornbread for supper.

But when I say "biscuits," you must not picture the low cylindrical things that most biscuits are, whether store-bought or homemade. Mama's did not look like that. They did not taste like that. I don't even especially like that kind of biscuit. Mama's quick bread was made with basically the same ingredients as others': flour; milk—buttermilk, clabber milk, sour milk, sweet milk, whatever she had, magically all tasting the same; lard or vegetable shortening, didn't matter which; baking powder, soda, and salt. The biscuits weren't flaky; they were substantial vehicles for butter, tasting more like risen rolls than standard biscuits. To this day nieces, nephews, grandchildren, and others remember this bread with dreamy looks in their eyes. It was truly the staff of life for us. One of my nephews who stayed with Mama and Daddy to go to high school in Virginia rather than in Baltimore used to stuff his pockets with Mama's biscuits before heading out to the bus. Once Daddy, then an elderly man, lifted him straight up off the floor and accused him of stealing bread, but he was only going to eat it himself, on the bus, or, like Napoleon Dynamite eating Tater Tots, perhaps in class.

Flour, standard white flour, we bought by the half barrel or by the hundredweight. Daddy would heft the 100-pound bag of flour onto his shoulder and take it to the flour barrel—a wooden barrel with a lift-off wooden top. Cornmeal, mostly white earlier, often yellow later, was bought mostly in 25-pound bags. Once, I recall taking our own corn to the gristmill over on Wolftown road, beyond Stanardsville, on the way to Madison. But that was not a usual event, because we did not ordinarily have dried corn: We didn't plant field corn like Uncle Ernest, who also planted wheat, and the sweet corn we ate as corn on the cob, cutoff corn, or roastin' ears.

I surmise that at least three factors contributed to Mama's unique biscuits. She always used the same bowl to make the dough, and it was not cleaned more than once a week. The bits of old dough probably had a yeasty effect. She always mixed the dough and shaped the biscuits with her bare hands, never rolling and cutting the dough, pinching each biscuit off and shaping it into a nearly perfect circle. We have yeast on our bare hands, and no doubt some transferred to the biscuit dough. Then the biscuits were cooked in the blazing hot oven of a wood cookstove. They came out of the oven a golden or darker brown, 2 ½ to 3 inches in diameter, a low convex curve to their tops—the perfect vehicle for butter, jelly and preserves, sausage gravy, whatever. Larry and I enjoyed them with bacon, raw onion, and yellow mustard. Slices of ham suited them just fine.

Of course, nobody ever wrote her recipe down, if recipe in the ordinary sense of the word even existed. She'd dump in some flour, slosh in some milk, gouge some fat out of the can with her fingers. She usually measured the baking powder and soda, rarely anything else. She'd pour a bit of salt into her hand, eyeball it, and affirm it right. Then she'd squish it all together, shape it into a comely ball, knead it, turn it, and pat it a bit, dust it with flour, and then start pinching off lumps. Magic!

Hazel's husband, Joe Clayson, of Baltimore Italian descent, nattered at Hazel to learn how to make Mama's biscuits, but she couldn't, though Hazel was a darn good cook. Joe loved them with butter and Old Virginia pineapple preserves when homemade was not available. Of all the people who tried, June in her prime probably came the closest, both on the biscuits and the cornbread. Still . . . .

As sound as he was on biscuits, Joe was totally unsound on cornbread. Like an unregenerate Northerner, he wanted sugar in Mama's plain cornbread, wanted corn cake! Now, Mama put a spoonful of sugar in corn muffins, as do I, but sugar in cornpone was anathema. I think that my corn muffins are good, but I've never equaled Mama's. Hers probably had more eggs than I put (two eggs for a batch of seven muffins), and no doubt more oil or other fat. Cooked in an oven as hot as one could get a wood stove, this bread I thought the best she made. These muffins she usually called "egg bread."

Regular cornbread had no eggs and not a jot of sugar. She cooked it on a cast-iron griddle, what Hispanics call a *comal* and use for tortillas. It was shaped into five or six pones by cradling a part of the wet mix back and forth, a hand-to-hand motion such as that used by Mexicans to make tortillas. When cooked in a fiery oven and slathered with butter, it accompanied cold vegetables just fine, with cold sweet milk on the side. Before bedtime we sometimes crumbled the leftover cornbread, if there was any, into a glass of milk and ate it with a spoon. Old-timers liked to eat cornbread in or with real buttermilk, not that acidy stuff that is cultured but what was left behind after churning, sometimes with little flecks of butter therein.

Mama never essayed yeast breads or light bread of any kind, though her sister, Aunt Lizzie, did. I'm sure that Daddy would not have eaten it. Admittedly the store-bought bread available in little country stores then was rather wretched stuff, and we almost never had it. Daddy called it "wasp's nest" and basically refused to eat it.

Churning butter was a ritual that I loved in childhood, not just for the outcome but for the process itself. Early on, we had one Jersey cow, which gives the richest milk, a Guernsey, and another. We milked twice a day, sometimes getting three gallons of milk at each milking. When we had lots of cream to be churned, we would skim it off the tops of gallon crocks plunged in the springhouse's water trough and use a crockery churn that held several gallons. A wooden dasher, inserted through a hole in the wooden lid of the churn, was dashed up and down, up and down, until the butter fat gathered and clustered together. With smaller amounts of cream, we would pour about a quart into a half-gallon jar and shake it for several minutes. When the butter "gathered," Mama shaped it into a ball with her hands and put it into a bowl, washing it with several changes of water, getting all of the liquid out by kneading and skooshing it. A bit of salt was added, and then the butter was shaped in a wooden mold and printed with a decorative design, or sometimes just left in a flattened ball to be used quickly.

Hazel, I think, bought us an electric churn somewhat later. It was quicker, of course, and had its own sort of magic—to be able to see the tiny dots of butterfat forming, then flecking, and quite suddenly coalescing into a big ball, whump! Sometimes we still used the shaking-in-a-jar method, especially with smaller amounts of cream, or to keep an idle child busy.

Daddy sits in the kitchen in the late 1950s, when it was at the front left of the house. The electric churn is visible on the table at the right and a bit of Mama's green-and-cream wood cookstove.

The mostly fat-free milk was left in the springhouse to sour, or if it was already sour (with wonderful real naturally soured cream on top, again so much better and sweeter than the cultured stuff), left to turn into thick clabber. Both were used for bread-making, and the clabber milk was used to make cottage cheese, though we always called it clabber cheese. To make homemade cottage cheese, Mama set the crock of clabber milk way back on the wood stove, near the water tank, until it separated into curds and whey. The nutritious whey went to the pigs. The curds were pressed in a wire strainer or in a cheesecloth, fluffed with a fork, salted and peppered. Then Mama poured lots of thin cream in, reconstituting and refattening the curds. That it was so much better than the store-bought kind goes without saying. We liked it with a bit of fruit or jelly mixed in. One of Mama's two brothers, Brother Mac, ate it with applesauce and Mama's biscuits. We did not make any other kind of cheese and did not make yogurt.

Daddy's most scathing contempt was kept for those farmers who sold their cream, which brought about the best price a farmer could get for anything, pound for pound, and made their families eat margarine. When cream was really abundant, in high summer, and before we had a freezer to handle surplus butter, we sold an occasional can of cream but never stinted or went without butter, sweet cream, sour cream, and everything related.

Milking time, summer of 1949: Mama is milking the Guernsey cow
Cherry; Fred is milking the Jersey cow Bossy; Kay looks on.

ii

Our food was, of course, quite seasonal, for other than flour, meal, dried beans, and sugar, in the early days we bought very few groceries and were mostly self-sustaining. Milk was much less abundant in the winter. Indeed, sometimes the cows had to be turned dry, waiting to be "fresh," to have a calf in the springtime when grass re-greened. The first milk that could be spared after the calf got its fill was often wild-oniony tasting. But this soon passed. Sometimes in late winter we had to make do with canned evaporated milk reconstituted. Still, calves, nearly always bull calves, were welcome, a cash crop that came in quite handy each year. Remember that Cherry's calf was the source of our washing machine.

Breakfasts were especially lavish. People needed the big-protein substance of a robust breakfast, for the hard work coming. In summer, at least early on, Mama and Daddy got up at 4 a.m., dawn in midsummer, and went to bed at full dark, 8 p.m. in those Eastern Standard time days. Daddy would work, mostly in the garden, in the cool for two or three hours before breakfast, which was almost always around 7 a.m. In winter, we got up later and stayed up later. Still, if one slept much past 8, as returning grown children sometimes wanted to do, Daddy, ever a strong man, would turn the double iron bed over on top of the sloth. I saw him do it to Roy. Roy seems to have brought out Daddy's most aggressive managing techniques: perhaps he liked Roy best of his five sons.

As I said, most of our dinners and suppers were vegetables, fruits, grain, and dairy only; at breakfast we were carnivores, and THE PIG, the beloved Anglo-Saxon and Irish PIG, was the factotum. After we butchered in the cold part of the fall, each breakfast likely had some form of pork— homemade, home-seasoned (not too much sage) sausage in patties or as sausage gravy; thick sidemeat or jowl bacon cut into rashers, skin on, sometimes with bacon gravy; fried tenderloin until it ran out, early; sometimes pork chops; on holidays or high occasions boiled shoulders or ham, unsmoked, sliced rather thinly but always with a thin ribbon of fat on the edge, which, of course, young'uns pulled off, foolish folk. We always had hams for Christmas and Easter and did not do much for Thanksgiving. I certainly never had turkey as a child and to this day think of it as the poorest of holiday traditions.

Pork that was deemed unsuitable for salt-preservation, such as sausage and tenderloins, was often canned. I can still see Mama struggling to get cold sausage out of a half-gallon jar to cook for breakfast.

The fattier parts of the pig—and pigs were bred to be much fatter and tastier back then—were rendered into lard, which was stored in big multi-gallon tin canisters with close-fitting lids. Lard was used for most pie crusts, and we sometimes had fruit pies for breakfast, certainly dried-apple fried pies in the fall and early winter. It was also the universal oil for most fried food. The residue of lard-making was cooked down to make cracklings, which Mama and others liked cooked in cornbread, but I didn't like cracklin' bread.

Those with different tastes, or stronger stomachs, than mine sometimes ate hog liver and onions, blood pudding (very rare, despite Mama's Irish ancestry), or chitlins (chitterlings). I had seen Mama and Oscar Steppe, the colored man about a quarter mile up the road, cleaning chitlins (hog intestines), and smelled them ("It's just the South, son."), so I never ate them. Kay saw some fried ones once and said, "Lord, I wouldn't eat them for $100." One of my brothers, probably Roy, said, "I'll give you a dime to eat one." Kay, ever ambitious of self-improvement and money to buy penny candy with, gobbled one down and got her dime—and then laughed at her brother for being such a simp.

Pig's feet—skin, gelatinous fat, and streaks of lean—most people would find disgusting (and I have certainly made them sound that way), but they are a "variety meat" of the pig that I liked as a child. I have not eaten any since then, but I liked them then. So shoot me. We did not eat them for breakfast but after long boiling, with seasoning, especially lots of black pepper. Pig trotters reminded me of *Pogo's* notorious chicken-foot jam.

Spareribs—we made no distinction for baby back ribs—were not eaten for breakfast. They were boiled, never baked or barbecued, and eaten at dinner. Of course we sometimes had fried chicken at dinner, especially for company, but nearly all meat—pork mainly—was eaten at breakfast.

We did not keep any cows for beef. Indeed, in the early days we never had beef. I can remember the first time I had beef, probably when I was about twelve. Some relative, most probably Aunt Bonnie, possibly Aunt

Lizzie, brought a cooked pot roast, without the vegetables. It seemed strangely stringy, foreign, odd-tasting.

Any meat or fish available we were likely to have at breakfast—from fried chicken to fried wild game to fried trout. (Mama, like Lynne Rossetto Kasper, thought nearly all food improved by frying.) Daddy would have already been working leisurely for a couple of hours, and the protein and calories both helped.

In addition to eggs—fried eggs for everyone except me; one scrambled one for me as a very little boy—we always had gravy, either plain milk gravy or bacon or sausage gravy. In the summer we always sliced tomatoes into the gravy but never had tomato gravy.

We had oatmeal every day for breakfast. Daddy wanted it thick; I've always liked it thin; we got it thick. Daddy would issue weird PRONOUNCEMENTS which he must have gotten from his mother's practice: "Oatmeal is supposed to be browned on the top." Bad enough that it was so thick, but browned and dried out too? With no broiler in the wood stove how is this to be achieved?

"Spoons are supposed to be put in a glass in the middle of the table. Take one if you need it." Mama always assumed that everyone NEEDED a spoon, and Daddy wasn't washing the dishes.

Once in a great while Mama would fix the children some cream of wheat as a mid-morning or mid-afternoon snack on winter days. Occasionally, we had store-bought dry cereal, either Kellogg's corn flakes (not Post Toasties—gackkk) or Nabisco shredded wheat, big biscuits, neither of which Daddy ate, to the best of my recollection.

Breakfast was finished with buttered biscuits and fried apples or jelly or preserves. Mama would fry green apples, such as the Early Transparent, by the time they were as big as golf balls, with some sugar and butter. Granddaddy Baugher had been something of an orchardman, and at least eight full-size apple trees, two pear trees, several peaches, a crooked quince, some plum trees, and any number of sour cherry trees, in addition to a Concord grape arbor, remained, diminishing over the years, except for the sour cherries, which only increased. It's odd that we had no damson plum tree, for that was Daddy's favorite preserves. We had to buy damsons from Yettie Walton, about a mile up the road. My favorite preserves were sour cherry, remaining so until this day.

Mama made preserves (the whole fruit) or jelly quite often, never jam (made of crushed or ground-up fruit), never using store-bought pectin like Sure-Jell. We ate massive quantities of preserves and jelly, especially the wild berries like strawberries, blackberries, black raspberries, and huckleberries. Most years we made apple butter, cooked in a large copper kettle over a wood fire from before dawn in the fall of the year until after dark. My sister Kay taught us the proper chant: "All around the sides and twice through the middle,/ That's the way to stir the apple butter kittle [pronounced that way]." Mama measured the seasonings carefully, opining that most people added too much of the cloves. She was OK with the standard amounts of cinnamon, allspice, and sugar. This apple butter we stored in gallon crocks mainly, milk crocks, covered with wax paper tied with string or twine. The apple butter was thick and very dark, so much better than even the best store-bought varieties. It kept just fine without being sealed through canning.

Grownups drank long-perked coffee at breakfast, which Daddy always saucered to cool it. He then drank it from the saucer. Occasionally, Daddy would decide that the coffee all tasted like stump water and would swear off it for a while. Mama, *pococurante* in this little matter, didn't seem to care one way or the other. Very occasionally she drank a cup of hot tea and, later, relished a cup of hot water. Children were allowed coffee, about half milk, only when we had fish, to guard against little bones, and the combination of fish and milk was sometimes deemed poisonous—as self-contradictory as this practice is.

iii

Dinners, especially in the late spring and summer, were full of garden produce and fruit. Spring onions, cucumbers, leaf lettuce, and tomatoes were always there on the table in season. June or "English" peas, green beans, lima beans—whether baby limas or speckled—always called butterbeans, green blackeye peas, beets—pickled with vinegar and sugar or just buttered, carrots, cabbage and coleslaw, squash—yellow crookneck or pattypan, not zucchini, new potatoes, and corn, corn, corn, were the main vegetables, with sweet potatoes later and sauerkraut made from the cabbage. Kay liked cabbage so well that she would eat it, leftover, for breakfast the next day. We sprinkled it with salt and ate a lot of it raw, sometimes without troubling to make coleslaw.

Mama frequently creamed vegetables of all kind, and there was always lots of pot likker. Her new potatoes were gloriously rich, thickened with cream, butter, and a bit of flour. Larry and I liked them best cold, with diced onion and sliced tomatoes. Bowing to Daddy's crotchets, she nearly always boiled potatoes. He did not particularly like mashed potatoes, though we had them often enough, with him quoting some country wag who had said, "Let whoever chewed them eat them." We had baked potatoes, of course, and roasted corn. From July on we had many, many ears of boiled sweet corn every day, lavishly buttered, salted, and peppered. And Mama cut corn off the cob and simmered it in milk. Sometimes we had vegetarian soup— good tomatoes, corn, butterbeans, onions, and carrots in a rich broth. With all of this vegetable bounty—sometimes five or six different vegetables at a meal—Roy had a hard time getting it all on his plate. He always spent many minutes arranging everything into a mountainous pile before demolishing his food. He was the shortest male in the family, and later the broadest, but he wasn't so in his teens.

Late in the season, Mama fried sweet potatoes, still my absolutely favorite way to eat these nutritious things. After they sweetened up a bit after being dug, she peeled and sliced them lengthwise and cooked them in butter and a bit of brown sugar. She liked the dry white-fleshed sweet potato, but everyone else preferred the orange. We also sometimes had light yellow-fleshed sweet potatoes. I never saw purple sweet potatoes then. During long winter nights we delighted in cooking regular potatoes and sweet potatoes too right on top of the wood stoves, in long, peeled slices that would caramelize, brown, and blister. These were always finger food. Both "Irish" potatoes and sweet potatoes we sometimes ate raw as snacks, though they are odd-tasting raw. When we had brush to burn, we roasted potatoes in just their skin in the ashes. We had no such thing as aluminum foil in the house. The peel was burned to a thick black crust, the insides a fluffy delight.

After regular potatoes were dug, turnips were planted in those spaces. Many were fed to the cows, and we ate lots of raw ones sprinkled heavily with salt. Mama liked them simmered in milk. The turnip greens we sometimes ate, and sometimes we had mustard greens or a bit of kale.

I don't remember ever having spinach or collards as a kid. Greens were always called "salad" or "sallet greens." Our chief variety was gathered wild, in late winter, from previously planted areas, where Upland Cress, as it's formally known, would spring up without planting. In southwest Virginia, it is known as "creasy greens." We always knew it as "cree salad." Greens were always boiled in lots of water for pot likker, with a bit of salt pork added, boiled and sometimes drained and refreshed until the bitterness was gone and they surrendered. We always had vinegar with greens, but our family did not add hot sauce, as many Southerners do.

In late summer, we made large—5-gallon or larger—crocks of sauerkraut. We sliced thinly many dozens of heads of cabbage, sprinkled it generously with salt, and then pounded it with a wooden cylinder or mallet right in the crocks. Plates weighted with rocks kept the fermenting cabbage beneath the brine. These crocks were put in the meathouse or in the corner of the garden in the shade of a sour cherry tree, with a tea towel tied under the plate to keep insects off. It stank ferociously but turned a rich amber that gave winter rewards. I have never learned to do anything more than tolerate store-bought sauerkraut, finding it rather nastily sour, imperfectly fermented, and almost unfoodlike. But Mama's sauerkraut, cooked long and slow in a bit of bacon grease in a cast iron pan, was golden, mellow, and delightful.

In the depths of winter, much of our dinner and supper protein came from dried beans, mostly pinto or blackeye peas, occasionally navy or Great Northern or limas, very rarely something like yellow eye. Beans had to be cooked for several hours, again with the obligatory bit of pork for flavoring, and often eaten with diced sour pickle, green tomato ketchup that Mama had canned, and diced raw onion. Mama sometimes canned piccalilli and chow-chow. Excellent pickles (and preserves too) were made of watermelon rind. Cling peaches, when we could get them, made sublime pickles. When pickles were a-making, the house smelled wonderful, all vinegary and spicy.

Lots of other canned goods varied the menu of potatoes and beans: canned corn, tomatoes, beets, applesauce, green beans (always, truthfully, called string beans), green limas, and carrots for soup. Most vegetables and fruits were done in a water-bath canner (Mama was afraid of pressure cookers, and how could you regulate them on a wood stove?) and were done in half-gallon jars, carrots always excepted. Other than tomato juice and tomatoes (technically a fruit but never so considered) our chief canned fruit was sour cherries (my absolute favorite, of course), blackberries, and applesauce. We had canned pears (no one's favorite) and some plums.

We had cooked apples, pears, and cherries sometimes at meals; but the fruit was eaten raw mostly or turned into pies. In early June, my all-time favorite, tart cherries, were turned into handsome pies in Pyrex dishes, cherry rolls, or deep-dish pies made in a cast iron skillet, sometimes with only an upper crust. Daddy's favorite pie was sweet potato. Larry's was blackberry, which Mama often cooked in a 12-inch cast iron pan with only a top crust. It was peach pie in August, mostly from orchard-bought peaches, for we canned many bushels of them. Mama's apple pies would win no beauty prizes, for they were often made with apples that cooked up. They were more like applesauce pies. All pies we children ate mostly with creamy milk poured over. Since the pies were usually warm or hot and frequently quite acidy—cherry and blackberry especially—it was a challenge to get just the right amount of cream and no curdle.

Cakes we ate less frequently, though we always had them for birthdays (until I requested cherry pie for mine) and for holidays. Daddy's favorite was coconut, almost always made, tediously, from fresh coconuts, which had to be cracked, the flesh peeled in chunks, then ground in a sausage mill. But let's face it: fresh coconut is better than store-bought pre-flaked. The kids' choice was devil's food. Daddy was one of those weird human beings who didn't like chocolate much, so all the more for us, since he had a tremendous sweet tooth when he did like something. At Christmas Mama always made, at the very least, the two foregoing ones and the universal favorite, expensive to make, Rocky Mountain cake, which used ground-up raisins, dates, oranges, mixed nuts, and fresh coconut as filling and icing. So good was it, in fact and memory, that, years later, Mildred and Patricia bought all of the ingredients to get Mama to make one for them. Most of the cakes were probably quite sweet, which almost no child objects to.

For some reason, this sweetness had to be accompanied by some contrast, usually pickles. I did not realize until later that most of the world did not eat cake with cucumber pickle or pickled peaches. Sometimes we had real whipped cream—a pain to make with a hand-turned rotary beater before we got an electric hand mixer—and sometimes we poured liquid cream over cake, *a l'Anglaise*, but often it was fruit—canned peaches or store-bought canned fruit cocktail.

Daddy grew wonderful melons in the sandy soil down near the spring—huge watermelons like Congo, Black Diamond, and Tom Watson. These were usually eaten in mid-afternoon, after cooling for a day in the water of the spring or the springhouse. Early on, he grew great big muskmelons, which we kids called mushmelons, greatly inferior, we thought, to watermelons. We couldn't understand how grown-ups liked them better than watermelons. Later, he grew delicious melons that we then called cantaloupe, the green-fleshed Rocky Ford being a great favorite. We always ate cantaloupe with salt and pepper but never put salt, or anything else, on a good watermelon, city-folk foolishness to doctor their poor melons, picked weeks ahead maybe. Cantaloupe we usually ate at breakfast, but they were so abundant that we often ate them again in the afternoon along with the watermelon bashes. Watermelon juice dribbled down our chins and arms, and we spat seeds at each other. We sometimes just broke open a watermelon in the field and gouged out the innards with our hands. The season was so precious and short-lived that we did not stand on manners and niceties when it came to melons. Daddy experimented with novel places to try melons, including way over the hill alongside a stream where most of the trees had been cut. It was partly shaded, but grew fine melons.

A watermelon-gouging: June, Larry, Kay, Roy, and niece Gail, about 1953.

August was also peach bounty month. Fred, Carl, and Roy usually picked peaches at orchards in Crozet, 8-10 miles south of Charlottesville. I think that they made fifty cents an hour (the same that I made in the sixties grading math papers for five different professors). At the end of long days, I'm guessing at least 12-hour days, they came home itching of peach fuzz and with their lunch boxes (the big arched-top black laborers' kind), filled—legally, I think—with real beauties, Elbertas, Hales, and the white-fleshed Georgia Belles. We ate them, like most soft fruit, in cream and milk. We always bought at least five or six bushels of peaches to can, I think at $2 a bushel. Hazel usually took some of her vacation from the Baltimore *News-Post* and came home to help with the canning of peaches. Nearly all were canned in half-gallon jars, some sliced and some in halves. The peach halves had to be arranged in the jar, pit side down, so that they looked pretty.

Some years we bought loads of apples to supplement what we grew, mostly the after-harvest gleanings in the big apple orchards near Winchester, Berryville, and Covesville, many of them owned by the Byrd family, big in Virginia politics and literature since colonial times. We usually roped in Aunt Lizzie's husband, Kyle Wood, or someone else with a big truck for hauling the many bushels we required. I remember one year, at least, having the meathouse filled to bursting with Staymans, Winesaps, the lopsided Yorks, Grimes Golden, and other old favorites that Daddy knew well from his father the orchardist. Many years we dried apples in the sun of autumn and stored them, first spread out on newspapers and then closed in large glass jars, stored in the unused back room upstairs, next to the flue that ran up from the kitchen stove, always warm and dry in winter. These were used mainly for fried dried-apple pies, eaten mostly at breakfast in the winter. I really liked them then but have had nothing like them in probably forty years.

We did not eat much store-bought fruit, but we certainly had bananas fairly often. The United Fruit Company, with all of its shady practices, nearly owned several of the Central American banana republics and the Caribbean portions of South America. By the early twentieth century, one could buy bananas, cheaply, in practically every little hamlet in America.

At Christmas time we reveled in store-bought produce. All old-timers had stories of getting one orange in their Christmas stocking when young.

But by the 1950s we bought 25-pound net bags of oranges, sometimes grapefruit, and the wonderful loose-skinned Dancy tangerines, now, alas, almost impossible to buy, with their tendency to produce only every second year. We always bought fresh coconuts at Christmas, for cakes and pies, and dried fruit, mostly raisins and dates, for baking. In the summer we often bought lemons, Mama making lemonade in one-gallon crock jars, so they must have been relatively inexpensive.

Christmas time also saw us with boxes and boxes of the more exotic nuts we could not find in the wild—almonds, pecans, English walnuts, and Brazil nuts. We cracked them around the wood stoves and threw the shells into the woodbox for kindling. Mama used the nuts for baking. The older children, out working in the world, often bought lots of this fruit, nuts, and enough candy—hard, filled, and soft—to founder Napoleon's army marching on Moscow. Daddy loved "French" candy, hard to find these days, and rock candy to put into his bottle of bourbon to be nursed along for months.

Mama very rarely made candy, something like peanut brittle on occasion, or cookies either, sometimes ginger snaps or something like them.

Our family were farmers in a very small way—that is, gardeners in a very large way. And we were hunter-gatherers, long after their heyday. Larry and I did not hunt, but our three older brothers and Daddy did. From their hunting, we ate mostly rabbits and squirrels, with a rare quail and ultra-rare pheasant. In my youth I saw no wild turkeys and only one deer, across the fields at the edge of the woods. The success of both species—indeed over-success—was to come later, the wild turkey's explosion due to human intervention and the deer's success mostly owing to suburbia with its lush planting, where non-hunters live. But I never ate any of either species then.

Rabbits and squirrels were skinned, cleaned, and soaked in salted water overnight and often parboiled and then battered in flour and fried, Mama's universal cookery. They were usually eaten at breakfast, though Mama sometimes made squirrel hash in a pot with lots of onions and black pepper, to be eaten at dinner. Both rabbits and squirrels were hearty and tasty provender, the squirrel somewhat more delicate than rabbit, which Europeans eat a great deal more than we do. When my brothers got a possum, they usually sold it, for fifty cents, I think, to the elderly Negroes who lived up the road, Bob and Doshie Blakey.

Most of the family were fishers, and Mama always fried the fish, dipped in cornmeal, often for breakfast. To my taste, the best-eating fish were sunperch, catfish, and rainbow trout. Others liked white chub especially. After thunderstorms, my brothers often caught eels. They were skinned and fried, like catfish, and tasted similar, though a bit sweeter and spongier in texture. We also sometimes had frog legs, very tasty. I'm now ashamed to say that my brothers gigged frogs—that is, speared them with an implement that looked rather like Poseidon's trident, though usually with just two prongs.

We knew most ordinary wild foods, but I've never tasted some, such as poke salad. Mama's fear of poisonous things made us steer clear of anything that had poisonous parts. We went in more for nuts and berries than the more exotic wild herbage. We especially longed for wild berries, and strawberries were the first of the year and first in our affection. In late May they were all around, especially in the half-shade where grass met trees. We usually picked them in containers that we could stick our snouts into and breathe in the ambrosial fragrance, one of the best the world has to offer. These strawberries are aptly named *Fragaria virginiana*. Years later, I was gratified to read that the 17th-century angler Izaak Walton said, "Doubtless God could have made a better berry, but it's equally doubtless that God never did." We ate them in cream with perhaps a bit of milk mixed in. When there were plenty, Mama made strawberry preserves, though capping them was a torture: they were so tiny. One woman we knew capped them as she picked, which was way too cold-blooded for our grasp.

For a few years, periodically, we had big tame strawberries in our garden, but strawberries tend always toward chaos, which Daddy would not endure in the garden, would not endure the tangled mass which he could not cultivate to keep weed-free. So he would rip them out.

Later came huckleberries, technically wild blueberries, and black raspberries, the latter especially sumptuous in cream and really good as preserves or jelly. Occasionally, Mama made black raspberry pies, fine-tasting but tougher than blackberries in a pie. I don't remember there being any wild red raspberries or wineberries either where I lived. Growing with the huckleberries was a similar bush that Mama always said was gooseberries, poisonous to eat. Of course they weren't gooseberries, which

I grow. They had leaves like the wild blueberries, but the bush and fruit were twice as large or larger. The berries turned a strange speckled pinky-green when ripe. To this day I don't know what they are, though I've paged through my 1500-page *Flora of Virginia*, recently published, the first since the eighteenth century. I always focused on July 4 as the target date for black raspberries and huckleberries.

In the latter part of summer, we sometimes found fox grapes, mostly by following our noses. These reddish-rust grapes perfumed the whole woods, but the vines snaked up trees, hanging thirty feet or more above. We had to cut the vines and drag them down through the limbs. They were scrumptious, the wild origin of the Concord, Catawba, and Delaware grape. But they were more perfumed and luscious than the cultivated varieties derived from them, and I delight in Concords. I've never tasted any grapes like them, though it's been over fifty years since I've had any. Worth growing, if I can find a source.

In late July and August, blackberries reigned, with more of those berries than any other, especially as second growth where trees had been cut. Some were really sweet—especially the dewberries that curvetted over the ground; some tended to the small and bitter. All made really good jelly and preserves, and pies fit for gourmets. Blackberries were so abundant that Mama canned dozens of half-gallon jars of them most years. Daddy would go out with two 2 ½- gallon water buckets and come back in an hour or two with them full. He was a very fast but quite slapdash picker: it took a long time to get rid of the leaves, twigs, and other debris—green berries included—from Daddy's raking fingers.

This found food did not have to come from our land. If people didn't pick the fruit that grew on their land, being too elderly or lazy or just not caring, then it was fair game. The only ones who ever objected were our next-neighbor, Alberta Shifflett, if we got piggy about wild strawberries on her land, which her two grown sons sold, or Elizabeth Shifflett, about a mile up the road, who would fire a shotgun at anyone she saw in her chinquapins unless one of her children was with the picker.

In the spring and summer we browsed from the bushes and trees such exotics as we could find, such as haws and serviceberries, which were known, confusedly and confusingly, as currants. But there were never enough of these to do anything except eat them out of hand.

In the fall came the nut bounty: chinquapins, little wild chestnuts, from champion second-growth large bushes or small trees, these not stored but eaten quickly, for they would not keep more than a day or so; hazelnuts, quite abundant down at the edge of the woods that bordered Uncle Ernest's flat; hickory nuts, those from the shagbark hickories with the best and biggest kernels; and black walnuts and butternuts, which had to be shucked from their outer covering, staining everything in sight, and dried for a while. All winter long we blissfully cracked our wild nuts at the woodpile, with hammer or hatchet back or axe. It was excellent protein, especially when meat was scarce.

After the first frost, we ate wild persimmons, shrunken and delicious, with large flat seeds. If you ate the persimmons before frost, even when they had turned orange, it was a mouth-puckering experience. I doubt that we ever gathered persimmons without chanting the old ditty "Possum up the 'simmon tree, raccoon on the ground./ Raccoon said to the possum, 'Throw some 'simmons down.'" Beyond the gate into Uncle Ernest's cow pasture, over toward Dan Collier's, were three tall and prolific persimmons. We ate the persimmons raw only, though they can be made into jam or puddings. I did not know of any paw-paw trees where I lived, so that native fruit was unsampled.

Apple trees gone to the wild over the centuries were fairly common, and we ate the knotty, strange varieties, though it might have been considered trespassing, our picking what we could find when we walked back from Durrette's River (again, Swift Run) and needed some refreshment in the heat of early autumn. Really good pears we usually snitched from Uncle Ernest and Aunt Ruby's tree, Bartlett-type pears that, if they did anything with, were destined for Aunt Ruby's ghastly pear preserves. We all knew that Aunt Ruby couldn't cook anything that came within leagues of Mama's, and we didn't even like Mama's pear preserves much. We had only hard pears that never ripened into the beauties that theirs did. But we felt guilty when we could see Aunt Ruby, ever sneaky, watching us from window's edge in the backroom of their house.

I've described our food as it was early in my life. It changed, almost certainly for the worse, as the years went on. We were less self-sustaining, there was more money in the household, and the house was infested with grandchildren. When I was in high school, Kay, working for a medical publisher and printer in Easton (Maryland) and Baltimore, sent home $20 a week—more ready money than we generally had and a big help in the 1950s. Older children had sent money home, in the country tradition, but this was far more regular and larger. Daddy started drawing Social Security when I was 16, and that monthly money, and age, made him less inclined to raise pigs. Mama was not to draw her pittance until ten years later.

A mentally ill son, a daughter-in-law who would watch a woman twice her age do work that SHE should have been doing, and all of this couple's offspring, all living at home now, drove our food further away from the wild and home-grown, more toward ground beef. And Mama grew older, tireder, slower, changing forever what she whipped up in the kitchen.

But in the glory days my mind's image of us as kids is that, when home, we were incessantly eating something, all day long. And yet we were basically all as skinny as whippets. I think of Roy as the stockiest one of us, and yet his high school graduation picture shows that he was quite trim then. Kay, whom Uncle Ernest, ever the nicknamer, dubbed Lard-Ass as a young child, was skinny like the rest of us through the school years. When I went to college, I was 5 feet, 9 ½ inches tall; yet I could not have weighed more than in the 120s. Indeed, we nearly all seemed impervious to calories until past the age of 30. Some of this was no doubt due to DNA, but much of it had to do with the fare that was ours, the eatin's we had and didn't have.

Chapter 4

Family Dramatis Personae, Center Stage

Central to my world, and apparently growing more important every day that I live, are my parents, both as a couple and as individuals. Each was an estimable person, but they made an odd couple. "Mutt and Jeff" Uncle Ernest called them in his most secretive, wryest, and meanest moments. I heard him, though he probably thought he said it *sub voce.*

At a casual glance they certainly looked different: he was 5'11" in his prime, and she never topped 4'11". He had all-but-black hair, not the color of coal or of ravens, rarely seen in European coloration, but black enough to be called black; she had ash blonde hair, fine and light, so that it was hard to tell when it started going gray. When they married, he was 29 years old; she, two months shy of 19 and seven months pregnant.

The only picture of Daddy as a young man that I know of, this
Baltimore studio portrait was taken in the late 1920s.

Pregnancy before marriage has never been a rarity, not during the
thousands of years before Shakespeare, not unknown to Shakespeare's
wife, Anne Hathaway, eight to nine years HIS senior, and not during the
hundreds of years since Shakespeare. Especially not rare in the Baugher
family, such an early start on a family need not be much of a drawback,
some minor embarrassments aside.

The fact about this early pregnancy that seemed most significant to me
as a full-grown adult was Uncle Ernest's reaction. He offered his younger
brother a sizable sum of money not to marry Mama. Now, I loved and
liked Uncle Ernest, but this is bastardly behavior, and I'm glad that my
father was a more honorable man than his elder brother, who was always
an asshole in such matters, with at least one of his sons as well as with
his brother. Apparently he thought that if a woman got pregnant before
marriage she wasn't worth marrying. I'm glad that I did not know of his

offer when I was young. When Daddy told three or four of us grown children about the incident, he closed with something like "Olga is worth five Rubys," Ruby being Uncle Ernest's chosen one.

Mama in a studio portrait in Baltimore, apparently taken at the same time as Daddy's portrait above. She said she had the mumps when the picture was taken.

I don't know how Mama, knowing of Uncle Ernest's action, and he got along, but they were neighbors. And he had let Mama and Daddy and their growing family live in a house on his land. Somehow they got along, due mainly, I suspect, to Mama's gentle temperament. As far as I could observe, Uncle Ernest always seemed a little uneasy in Mama's presence if Daddy wasn't there. I know that they both remembered the action. As Mama herself always said, "I can readily forgive, but I never forget."

The greatest contrast between Mama and Daddy was not physical but temperamental. He was hot-tempered and often angry to the point of derangement and had apparently always been so. Again, Uncle Ernest: "I don't know what's wrong with Raleigh; he's always been that way, ever since he was a kid." He didn't seem to inherit his temper: Granddaddy Baugher was apparently a relatively gentle man. Mama liked and respected him. And I never saw anything hot-tempered in Grandma Baugher, though she died when I was nine years old and I didn't see her much.

Mama reported that Daddy had said when he was younger he was often mad as hell and didn't even know why. Still, he was very tender-hearted. Though he would get steaming mad and treat people badly, especially his wife and children, he would feel guilty thereafter and make some stumbly attempts to make amends.

Mama was very slow to anger, rarely angered. She boasted that when she did get angry she was "as mean as two black snakes." I never saw it, and I suppose that she meant black racers, for, though they are not poisonous any more than other black snakes are, they are very tetchy and bitey. Mama was not.

Mama could be obdurate and get her back up but mostly to speak well of people to contradict anybody that spoke ill. I imagined that if anybody said anything unduly harsh about Lucifer himself, Mama would defend him: "Now he's a hard worker." She mainly contradicted Daddy—not TO him and not so he could hear, but later, mostly to the children.

Central to my parents' difficulties with each other was sex. To think of one's parents' sexuality is not wise, and I'm as behindhand at wanting to do it as the next person. However, I found out something much, much later that made sense of things in my childhood. Obviously, they had been highly sexual beings—nine children in seventeen years, one started well ahead of the decorous time. However, something happened. Shortly after I was married my mother told Mae, my wife, apparently as warning, that when I was born the obstetrician told her that to have another child would kill her. I doubt that it was true; it may have been his way of doing his little part, mostly too late, for population control, for Mama was not yet 36 when I was born. He pointed out to her what a misfortune it would be to her children to be bereft of a mother. And so her tubes were tied.

Mama, always religious in a very literal way, taking the injunction to be fruitful and to multiply to heart, seemed quite disturbed by the thought of sex without the possibility of procreation. She may have lost all sexual desire. No wonder I stayed in my parents' bed so long, and though there were already eight children for the four double beds upstairs, and I was odd baby out, I did not have to stay in my parents' room as long as I did. It was not fair to use me in this way, and I sometimes suspected that Daddy favored Larry over me—and this might have been cause enough—but he warmed to me later, and of course I knew nothing of the other matter at that time. One more icky item on this subject: I think, but do not know, that Daddy sought consolation elsewhere. And I think that my sister Violet, at least, thought that she knew more. At any rate, at Violet's funeral her daughter read a list of Violet's loves: her mother, always; her father and husband, sometimes. Enough of this, and "Ewwww."

To shared things: I believe that Mama and Daddy were the two hardest-working people, physically, that I have ever known. Daddy used to boast of being able to work other people under the table, and this boast seems warranted. Some of his old confreres in road construction and shipbuilding said as much. I remember Mama's cousin John Long saying that Raleigh Baugher was the hardest-working man he ever knew. And of course Mama demurred since he had not worked in a public job then for ten or fifteen years. All part of the contradictions. Mama also worked hard—hand washing clothes, cooking, milking, and on and on, doing much of the raising of two generations, and she often was doing it when Daddy was dozing over the newspaper with the baseball Game of the Day on the radio.

Both were intelligent but not very educated. Daddy did not do the last year of high school, secondary schooling then lasting but eleven years, and Mama, living farther from any possible school, and having nearly drowned going to Celt, finished only four grades. She honored learning and always wanted at least one child to be a teacher. I finally fulfilled that wish. I remember that my high school classmates George Lamb and Kennon Peyton were there when Marguerite Stephens, an English teacher and librarian who had taught most of the Baugher brood, said, "All of those Baughers are smart. And the McDaniels too." Kennon queried, "What about Roy?" Mrs. Stephens said, "Oh, he's smart in a different way."

Daddy read a great deal but mainly trashy stuff—no, not trashy, just formulaic—like Erle Stanley Gardner and Zane Grey, but really anything that his cousins or nephews brought to him after reading them. Included in this reading would be an occasional racy novel, such as one by Frank Yerby, that set my pulse racing with the hint of the unknown. You may be sure that I surveyed every book that came into the house, especially the joke books, with their softcore porn humor. Daddy read any college novel that I brought home at Christmas break and read *Hamlet* when I praised it, asking some very pertinent questions about what happened. Mama rarely read anything except a few magazines and the newspaper, keeping abreast of the latest doings of Ingrid Bergman, and she would fall asleep in a straight-back kitchen chair with the newspaper dangling. We had two newspapers a day, our subscription to the Charlottesville *Daily Progress*, traded every day with Uncle Ernest for his Washington *Times-Herald*, which became the *Post*. We got the Richmond *Times-Dispatch* on Sunday.

Daddy was honest to a fault. Indeed, I always got the impression that Mrs. Early, the doyenne of Celt, thought that he was the most honest man she ever knew. He sometimes cut pulpwood on shares from the huge land holdings of the Earlys, and she deferred to Daddy in every particle of calculating how much she was owed. She knew that if farthings had still been in use she would get what was due her down to the last farthing, and he had a really good head for mathematics and figgering. Part of this honesty was a fairly brutal tactlessness. No one ever had the nerve to point out to him that he didn't have to VOLUNTEER to say every single blasted thing that he thought.

Mama, an unusually good and Christian woman, told little fibs much of the time in order to hide the full truth of things from Daddy so as not to have to hear him fuss and rant. Most of the fibs were those of omission, not commission. Her favorite Biblical quotation was "Blessed is the peacemaker." She was blessed a thousandfold. For instance, Daddy never knew that Violet married a man, Bill Burns, who had a full family from a previous marriage and that he was 17 years older than Violet. Mama was afraid that Daddy would never let Bill set foot in the house again. Bill riled Daddy at the first meeting, big idea man telling Daddy how to run the farm and that he should bulldoze the hill cow pasture above the spring to flatten it out. "The fool wants me to ruin our spring."

When Daddy got angry with his brother Ernest, which happened rarely, he'd land on the fact that Uncle Ernest was four or five inches shorter than Daddy. Daddy would call him a "bottle-assed bastard." That's pretty representative.

A wild man in his youth, emulating his wastrel Uncle Johnny Lamb, Daddy was a hard drinker early and apparently a bootlegger with Uncle Johnny in the 1920s, though I never heard of this venture until I was nearly 70. When he became a family man, he essentially gave up drink except for one bottle of whiskey a year and a very rare bottle of beer, which he always drank in a glass, salted. Like his brothers, and like almost all amateur and professional baseball players of the early twentieth century (he loved baseball and had apparently played it well when young) he chewed tobacco all of his adult life, and he would smoke a stogie if someone like his nephew Aubrey or his former next-neighbor Ernest Davis Shifflett gave him one. For a short while he affected a pipe, but it just didn't take.

Daddy, like Uncle Ernest, was an irreligious blasphemer most of his life. According to Mama, Uncle Ernest wrote very pious letters to Grandma Baugher from the foxholes of France in World War I, but all of the years that I knew him he was quite skeptical and cussed nearly as much and as well as Daddy. Daddy, having had run-ins with thuggish labor unions when he worked in Baltimore during WW II, was rather conservative politically, in the honorable Dwight Eisenhower fashion, not in the batshit crazy Republican fashion so prevalent today. One of Daddy's greatest pleasures, still when I was of an age to remember, was cussing FDR and Eleanor Roosevelt and Harry Truman. I remember one time at table Daddy picked up the pepper shaker and stared at it with his wild hazel eyes ("Has Daddy snapped?" we wondered.) Then he spoke as if soliloquizing: "That Goddamn Harry Truman! It's getting so a poor man can't afford to buy pepper!" I don't think he ever knew how scary-funny he was.

Sometime in his 60s or early 70s Daddy got religion and joined the Baptist church, Swift Run, which was Mama's church only a hundred yards or so from her homeplace. He went for the whole schmear—full muddy river dunking in dress clothes. I wasn't there, but I was there to hear Mama regale two of his sisters, Lucille and Dolly, and, I think, some of Mama's relatives all laughing and really enjoying the telling. When the Baugher women of Daddy's generation got together, Daddy, an enigma of a man, was the chief subject of family talk always. Mama finished up big:

"And then the preacher said, 'Man, kiss your woman!' And he did!" The laughter and delight were unparalleled in Mama's story-telling.

Uncle Ernest was also vastly entertained and made sneeringly funny, profane remarks. And Daddy still cussed, of course, but age and maybe some religion cooled it a bit.

Mama talked a lot about the need for everyone to be "babtized." As far as I know, she won one convert only: my brother Carl was baptized and joined the church. I was conventionally pious, I suppose, especially at Christmas. Kay and I and, I think, Larry, sometimes, went to church at Mt. Paran Methodist Church with Miss Towne for a while. This involved a drive of several miles on dirt roads over in Albemarle County, real washboard roads leading down to the sideless Scribner's bridge, up by Pete LeTellier's house, and then back into Greene County. It was probably just a two-mile walk through the fields, over by the Davis place where Aunt Ruby spent her younger years, with Bea and Boss Davis.

All of the hoopla in the Baptist church about coming forward while "Just As I Am" went through its ninety-first singing, just alienated and embarrassed me. Religion as it was practiced in general did embarrass me. When we were young, Larry and I were exposed to cousins Leon and Nancy's demonstrating the recitation of the Hail Mary that they had recently learned. They would have been angry and mortified to know what we thought, and may be so now, but the truth will out: They were as proud as could be of their accomplishment; Larry and I thought this rigmarole the height of silliness and were mortified to hear it. My two oldest sisters, Hazel and Violet, became staunch Catholics, and June for a while was under the spell of Jehovah's Witnesses, and Larry listened to Herbert W. and Garner Ted Armstrong on the radio, but many of us were infidels and heathens, as Peggie Calhoun (later Byars) always told me I was at college.

Mama, on the other hand, was always singing old-timey hymns while she happily worked around the house. At best, her voice was quite erratic and defective, but I loved hearing her sing. Phrases of her songs still racket about in my head: "Tempted and tried, we're oft made to wonder . . ."; "Keep your hands upon the throttle and your eyes upon the rail . . ."; "On a hill far away . . . ."

She didn't go to church very often, for it was four or five miles away now, and we had no wheels. But revivals and lawn parties at church were cause for revelry and finding a way. She'd visit any country church holding a lawn party, and a cakewalk out on the grounds was bliss itself. She loved the old-time pump organs still to be found in a few country churches in my youth but disdained the high theatrics of the pipe organ. She was clearly Low Church all the way.

Mama always said that she liked a string band, by which I think she meant old-time mountain music. I don't know whether Daddy ever took her dancing in her teens and before the babies came, but she could still do a mean few minutes of the Charleston in her middle years when her children egged her on. Her Aunt Jenny reputedly was Queen of the County in dancing solo on a big rock. That's how Mama described it, though I had a hard time picturing it—maybe some sort of Irish dancing. June, who loved cutting a rug, must have understood, for her eyes glowed at the telling, and she named her daughter Jenny.

The most important fact about Mama and Daddy both is that despite their differences and despite the occasional uproar of the home, it was clear that they both loved all of their babies, that they would do whatever needed doing to see that we were well fed and that we lived a rich and wildly free country life, once below a time. They knew instinctively that the richest childhood anyone could wish for was one without the crush of worldliness and materialism, one full of the oblivion that Dylan Thomas found at Fern Hill, though of course neither ever heard of Dylan Thomas. They had gotten out of Baltimore as soon as they could and headed back to Greene County and their homes.

Next to my parents, of course, my brothers and sisters were the most important people in my childworld. Some of the adult Baugher children felt the full shadow, to switch poets, of the prisonhouse of adulthood much more than others, but let's go back to an earlier time and look at the large cast. Sour notes will intrude, but—and I don't think I'm romanticizing or sentimentalizing—we loved home and being there; all nine of us always went back home, often, and for as long a period as we could manage.

Like most happy families of children, we fought a great deal and teased and insulted each other. But we enjoyed each other, we played games as if doing so were our vocation, and we liked each other, mainly. We all shared beds with our siblings coming up, and you can't share a bed for long and loathe someone.

Most of us, if not all, were walking paradoxes—not the ineffable, holy kind of paradox uttered with such reverence by my college professor Robert Goldsmith, but loosely gathered bundles of contradictions sticking out at weird angles.

Until I ruined the balance and the symmetry, our family came thus: two daughters, two sons, one daughter, one son, one daughter, one son. Then I came. Hazel, born the nineteenth of November 1926, eleven days after my mother turned 19, and Violet, born the twenty-eighth of September 1928, I know least, for they were both gone from home, 17 and 15 years older than I was, before I can remember.

Hazel was the hottest-tempered and most generous spirit of all the children. Mama told the story of her trying to follow Daddy to work in Baltimore when she was two-ish. After being reprimanded several times, she picked up a broomstick and shook it at him, "Mean Daddy, mean Daddy, mean Daddy." This continued: she was always ready to have a go at Daddy in disputes about Catholicism or anything else, often up in arms about some personal cause, mainly ones growing out of something that she had misunderstood from the outset. She was the only one in the family that called Mama "Mother," and she always tried to be posh above her means. As far as I know, she felt most keenly of all the children the lack of money back on the farm. She married a man who was generous early but turned into a miser. To get the luxury she craved, she would later disport herself wildly with credit cards, but it must be said that she used them mostly to give to others, lavishly for her means.

I can believe that Hazel, who called her high school teachers, always, names like "Old Lady Parrott" or "Old Lady Moyers," was a handful at William Monroe. She graduated fifth in her class, the only girl in the family who was not salutatorian, and always accused one of the "old ladies" of cheating her out of higher honors.

She was devoted to both of her parents, even "mean daddy," and came home on some at least of probably every vacation she ever had, though she and Joe traveled a lot when young. She came home to help with canning tomatoes or canning peaches, whatever. She worked in payroll at the Baltimore *News-Post*, always second banana to the *Sun*. She remained childless but gave, gave, gave to all of her younger siblings and later to her many nieces and nephews, having to pry it from Joe Clayson's fingers, figuratively speaking. This is the Hazel of my youth—and Joe was generous also at first—and I won't go beyond that period.

Mama with Hazel and Violet at the bungalow in Baltimore
where they lived for a while. Summer of 1929.

In my youth, and indeed later, I knew Violet the least of my siblings. She came home to take care of the family when I was a small boy, when Mama was in the hospital, I think for a gall bladder operation. She handled the work smoothly, but the chief item that I remember is a mother hen's setting up the alarm just outside the house when a black snake was trying to get her baby chicks. At least that was the chicken's interpretation of events. Insouciantly, Violet dispatched the snake with a hoe, and the chicks lived to lay.

I have said earlier that Violet fled the farm after getting a beautician's certification. Most of her visits home are associated in my memory with her giving "perms" to my mother and sisters out in the side yard, under a black walnut tree and sour cherry trees, the reek of the lotions assaulting my nose.

She married young. Her oldest child, Gail, named, I find, in honor of

Miss Towne, who liked the name, was born when I was 7 ½. Gail spent long parts of some summers at the homeplace from the time she was three, ubiquitous in photos from the early to mid-fifties.

That Violet was feisty, humorous, eccentric, and hard-working is easily gathered. The best evidence I have is hearing Gail give a kind of eulogy at the funeral home, honoring her mother in the presence of Violet's brothers, children, grandchildren, and great-grandchildren. She's the only one of my siblings that I know to have admired Emanuel Swedenborg.

Gail told of Violet and Hazel's being cruised by a couple of would-be pickup artists in Baltimore when they were young. Violet, not breaking stride, pulled out a fake big nose with glasses and a moustache as the car pulled up. They sped away, and Hazel lamented Violet's driving them off.

And this, the most characteristic anecdote I can repeat to etch Violet's character early and late: a devout Catholic, with at least six children then, possibly all seven, she went to work at the Baltimore post office, to give her children more chances in life. Once, she was hit upon by a smooth, smooth, smooth seducing snake, "How about a little bit?" She drew herself up to her full height—an even 5 feet—and said at once, turning his words against him, "Well, Goddamn, if a little bit is all you have to offer, then no thanks."

That is Violet.

Violet, about 19, and our first cousin Eddie Estes.

Fred's is perhaps the hardest character to limn. Born the seventeenth of January 1930, he was a sweet, sweet teenager when I first knew him, but with the seeds of paranoid schizophrenia within, already a bit evident when I backread. The firstborn male, he probably felt the brunt of Daddy's giving him hard tasks more than anyone else later. Mama was inclined to coddle him, as he no doubt needed, and I would judge that his relationship with Daddy was exacerbated by that.

He shows himself full of joy in a few pictures from his teens—when he is holding his dog Rover, when he is riding a bicycle, when he is smushing an Easter egg into his mouth with sister Hazel looking on benignly from the doorway. But many pictures show him with furrowed brow and a wounded look in his pale blue eyes, his wavy blond hair either meticulously coiffed or in a shaggy mop.

Fred eating an Easter egg, 1948, Hazel looking on.

Like Hazel, he was as generous and as loving to his siblings as well could be. He made sure that Larry and I always had at least one bicycle between us. He spent $75, a big sum in the mid-50s, on a big purple bicycle for us, money hard won in construction.

By 1945 Bill Monroe had essentially invented the bluegrass sound, and it was the delight of Fred's life. When Violet came home, the two of them, less than sixteen months apart in age, the smallest gap in the family, the closest of pals early on, sang bluegrass duos down under the clothesline behind the meathouse. He bought a motorcycle—all of us always crazy for some kind of wheels—and Violet, on a home visit, got on it and tore down the dirt/gravel road that ran by our home. The loose gravel where she turned, down at the road through the woods to Uncle Ernest's, made her come a cropper, hurting and bloodying herself thoroughly, but she pushed the cycle back home. She might have been seriously injured. I can't remember when the motorcycle went, but it wasn't there long.

Toward the end of the Korean war, Fred was drafted, despite his bad eyes, and was stationed in Okinawa. He had had brilliant report cards at Celt Elementary, but he did poorly in high school, even for Marguerite Stephens, who really liked him and was solicitous in asking me about him many years later. Daddy let Fred drop out, after ten grades, and Carl with him, only finishing nine grades. Mama hated that and considered Daddy, who was always coming all paterfamilias on us, as derelict in duty. It probably made little difference for Fred. One Army picture shows him with two drinking, carousing friends with a woman hanging on one of them and Fred standing to the side, with furrowed brow, unsmiling, mental pain evident in every line.

When he came home, it was evident before long to most observers that something big was wrong. He told nasty sexual jokes that he had learned in the Army, and he rolled out all of the Japanese curse words that he had learned, laughing in a way that I found creepy. He got such laboring work as he could find around Charlottesville, bought a '54 Chevy truck and then a '56 Chevy Bel Air and courted and impregnated a young woman from near Scottsville, in Fluvanna County, Ruth Townsend, who worked at the supermarket in Charlottesville where Roy was a meat cutter. Ruth was tall, affable, easy to talk to, rather nice-looking, slightly resembling the young Queen Elizabeth II. And she had a lot to put up with in facing Fred's increasingly serious incapacity. However, as it became ever more evident that Fred could not hold a job, as the babies piled up and she did nothing to help matters, and as it became evident that they had no place to live but at the homeplace, her parents being unwilling to help except for very short periods, life became hard at home. It was hard for Larry and me, the only children still left at home, to give up our roles as lords of the household.

It was soon evident that Fred would be in and out of mental hospitals and V. A. treatment centers off and on, that he would not get better, even with horrific electro-shock therapy, and that he could live at home only under heavy medication, a shadow of himself. Daddy sold them an acre of land for $100, and they moved out beyond the barn, but two of the children were so attached to Mama and Daddy by then that they never moved, and nearly all of them ate at our home at least two meals a day.

Larry and I were angry about the home situation, our last couple of years of high school blighted at home. However, in later years I must admit that the nieces and nephews were a pleasure to play rounds of cow pasture golf with, to play all of the family games with—from Setback to Stud Poker, and for Larry to play touch football with and take fishing. Now, one of those nephews owns 40-plus acres of the homeplace and has turned it into a beautiful horse farm. The land itself, now partly bulldozed, the spring being no longer used, looks very handsome, better than it ever has, but who wants to admit this?

Carl, born the twenty-fourth of October 1931, was Fred's shadow during their teen years. They hunted, fished, and trapped mink and muskrat—to sell their hides to make spending money—together. They biked together. They each had a dog and seemed the main owners of the big black and white tuxedo cat, Monroe, looking surly when he is posed for pictures with Rover and Spot.

Carl had more trouble with academics than anyone else in the family. Mama says that he ran around as a very small child proudly spelling "cat" for all listeners: "C, T, cat." When he was in school at Celt, the multiplication tables were his nemesis. Mama knew that she had to go through his clothes carefully, for every pocket contained scraps of paper with the "times" tables written on them.

He was an inveterate tease. We all dubbed him Tom Marshall, Jr., after the man who lived a fraction of a mile down the road, the grandfather of Jimmy and Kenny Marshall, buddies of Larry and me. But he had no real meanness in him, unlike old Tom Marshall. Clearly Carl was a nice guy.

An unfortunate malapropist, he made us laugh and then would say "What? What?" when we whooped. One of my favorites was "Look at

Daddy over there, just salting his apple sauce down with sugar." Some of my siblings—Violet, Carl, and Roy—had strange pronunciations even into adulthood, as did Mama. My favorite of Carl's was "CUKE.a.mer" for the garden cucurbit, and it was his nickname for me for many years, I don't know why. Was I cool?

My three older brothers frequently had wild animals as pets, probably because they had killed the parents while hunting. I think that Carl was the main zoo-keeper. They had really tame baby squirrels, baby possums as cute as a bug's ear, and baby quail, with full-grown mallards later. They made elaborate runs for the squirrels out of hollow sections of a tree and whiled away many a happy hour contriving things for their pets.

Carl between Roy and Herman P. Shifflett, friend of Carl and
Fred. Larry, Glynn, and Kay in front. April 1951.

When Carl was pumping gas at his job in Charlottesville, he seemed content. When he worked at Bethlehem Steel, he seemed content. He married and fathered three sons, raising two of them by himself after the divorce.

Outside the scope of this memoir but worth noting: after he retired he moved back to the homeplace. It was still quite primitive living, but he said that it was the happiest day of his life. He died there in his 83rd year.

June, the fifth, the middle child, was born the twenty-eighth of January 1934. She may have been the greatest paradox of all the Baugher paradoxes.

Opinions will vary of course, and I'm not here to wound the feelings of descendants, but I always thought June in her youth the prettiest and, in an abstract sense, the smartest of all of my siblings. But she didn't seem to have a lick of worldly sense and would fall for every sham intellectualism she encountered. First it was astrology; then it was being a Jehovah's Witness and pointing out all of the bogus origins of most things of mainstream Christianity; then it was adoring some man that everybody else could see was a slimeball.

Like all of my sisters, she should have gone to college, giving some context to her bright enthusiasms. None did, for the tradition had been lost in the twentieth century, after centuries of Baughers (actually *Bägers*) being well-educated Lutheran ministers. But perhaps that tradition was for the eldest sons only. Clearly we were not from the eldest-son line of Johan Georg Bäger, the first American of the Baugher line.

In all of the family photos, most taken by Joe Clayson from 1948 on, June is always the one with her arms around Larry and me, with her arms around Kay, with her arm interlaced with Roy's. She was a loving person, and she probably loved Daddy more than any other one of us. I never knew her to do a mean thing, certainly not to me. When I went to college, Roy owed her money. She said, "Pay the debt back by sending the money in installments to Glynn." She wanted me to have spending money without having to work so hard.

June, Kay, and Glynn in the broomsage above our spring.

A sweet and kindly person, though rebellious toward Mama when young ("It's my life," etc., etc.), she grew to be Mama's most loving fan. Buffeted by her own kindly nature and bad enthusiasms, she gave birth to an illegitimate daughter, Jenny, when I was fourteen. Back then, in the fifties, this was a great stigma. I've never seen Daddy so hurt, lying on the bed and sobbing, this hard-as-iron man, when Kay told him.

June was a skilled linotypist, her fingers flying across the keyboard, working for the Michie law firm in Charlottesville and later for a medical publisher and printer in Maryland. When Larry and I were still young, she married a big, shambling, handsome, stupid man, France Deaton, from Toccoa, Georgia, who always wanted to talk about intellectual matters with me. I didn't like him and had nothing to say to him. I am sure that he abused her, both physically and mentally. She had the strength to boot him out and resumed her name of Baugher.

June taught all of her nieces and nephews within reach to fish. She developed what was called a mental illness in her middle years, though it seemed utterly different from Fred's and to me always seemed to be just what was then called "a nervous breakdown." Heavily medicated, on disability, she later bought a modest home for herself, her daughter, and grandchildren, quit smoking on the umpteenth try, wrote mostly bad poetry with an occasional thrillingly good line and fine haiku, and loved playing word games with Larry and me. I never knew a child who didn't like her, and Larry and I always had her utmost loyalty.

Roy, born the twenty-sixth of September 1936, has been named more often, probably, so far in this memoir than any other sibling. Especially contradictory, he was the funniest of us all, but unfunny when drinking, perhaps the sneakiest of all (Aunt Bonnie called him a snake in the grass), very smart in early schooling, just skimming by later, and the greatest horndog in the family, pursuing, as I said earlier, every pretty girl who didn't pursue him. He was vain of being told that he looked like Elvis Presley once that phenomenon erupted, but really only his hair had some likeness. More would-be lovers pursued him than all the rest of us combined.

Roy on his bicycle at the plum tree at the bottom of the front yard; Fred on his; cousin Eddie Estes; Glynn, probably, running up through the yard.

The reason must have been his confidence. He was the only one of us ever to appear in a full-length class play. He was cast as a twin to Nina Shifflett, a pretty dark-haired classmate. He flung around the titles of works being read for class just as if he had read the whole works. I remember especially his talking about [Less Miz.er.a.bulls]—that's how he said it, the first time I had ever heard of *Les Miserables*. Of course, I set myself the task of reading it myself later. But I read it all, on my own. He would talk about the Shakespeare plays read for class—and we had one each year of high school—again as if he knew what he was talking about.

He prided himself, like Daddy, on how hard he could work, calling himself a "hard roller." He finished high school, unlike his two older brothers. Like them, he tried to work in Charlottesville and became a skilled meat cutter at Stop and Shop supermarket. But Charlottesville just did not pay enough, anywhere, for ambitious young men. He headed to Baltimore like everybody else, and longed to be back in the country all of his life. His early pride was his first car, a used light blue 1953 Mercury. Let's leave him tooling around in it.

Roy and Juanita, recently married, at home, 1958.

Kay, born the fifteenth of August 1939, was Grand Pooh-Bah of play for the triad—her, Larry, and me. She started the plan of making bicycle paths all through the deep-piled leaves of Uncle Ernest's woods. She bought and made picnics for us of potted meat on crackers, Kool-Aid in half-gallon jars, and all the penny candy she had, and she always had it. She always had money, for she would hot-foot it over to Uncle Ernest's whenever she saw any of his children from Baltimore go down the dirt road, gone to babysit Harry's children, Ray's children, Frances's children.

She knew skip-rope rhymes, apple-butter incantations, the rules of all games we ever encountered, where to find haws, the relationship of everybody to everybody within quite a few square miles, the words of every old chestnut song from school choir classes—everything from "Reuben, Reuben, I've been thinking . . ." to probably dozens of songs by Stephen Collins Foster.

Mama, Glynn, Larry, and Kay, 1948.

She had deft fingers: she could thread the tiniest-eyed needles made, and Mrs. Davis, the high school biology teacher, always got Kay to peel raw eggs so that the membrane just inside the shell was still intact.

In the summertime our older brothers would drive us to Charlottesville for one of their workdays and give us money, the three youngest of us, to progue (Mama's wonderful word, meaning to poke, to pry, to rummage, to snoop) around the streets all day. Kay was chief, mainly picking the movies we would see in the afternoon, lying to get Larry and me in at children's rates, understanding the Greek ice cream vendor—or pretending to—at the Lafayette Theater. It played Grade B or lower movies, unlike the Paramount and the Jefferson, so we never went there, but no day hitting Woolworth's, Leggett's Bargain Basement, and all the movies we could manage—sometimes even to the University, many, many blocks away near the University of Virginia— would be complete without the Greek man's vanilla ice cream cones. In memory at least, Ben and Jerry couldn't hold a candle to him.

With her deft fingers flying perhaps even faster than June's, Kay became a monotypist at the same medical publisher and printer.

Kay was my closest bud in the family next to Larry. She will always be Queen of the Revels, the authority on all things fun.

Larry was born on the eighteenth of January 1942; I was born on the third of October 1943. Thus we were about 21 months apart, but I was bigger for my age than he was for his. By the age of 6 or 7 I was about the same size and thereafter was taller and bigger until we were in our 20s. We hung together just about all of the time and seemed to have one name between us, sometimes Larrynglynn, sometimes Glynnenlarry. We even ate hard-boiled eggs together, one eating only the yolks, the other only the whites. Uncle Ernest, borrowing from Rod Brasfield, Minnie Pearl's male counterpart on radio's Grand Ole Opry, called me Pete and Larry Repeat (I was taller by then). Though we looked nothing alike, many people thought us twins because we were in the same grade. In high school Mrs. Stephens could never remember that I was younger; when talking to me, she called Larry "Baby brother."

When young, we were both as shy as whippoorwills: If we saw strangers drive in, we would dart behind the meathouse, scramble under the barbed-wire cow pasture fence, skirt the main garden, and make it into Uncle Ernest's woods to watch whether we wanted to come out. If the visitors looked like total strangers, we would run away even if Mildred and Patricia were visiting. They understood and would even help us get away. If we had had our complete choice, we would have seen no one but family and close neighbors before starting school, and not some of them. (Elderly female relatives had a habit of dragging us from under beds to kiss us.)

Larry at home, boy of summer, 1949.

Though Larry was quite bright, he never particularly liked school. I was the whippoorwill that could be ushered into daylight, Larry not so much. Mad for baseball from a sprat, he would have gladly spent most days hitting rocks with a homemade bat. He kept statistics on paper of his fantasy leagues and batted for all of the players, giving a play-by-play broadcast as he swung. I've seen him do this for hours in a row.

We both loved cats from an early age. Mama nearly always had cats and kittens around the house. Some would follow her when she went a-milking. Some would spaniel her at heel while she made bread, reaching up to beg raw biscuit dough. Larry, not yet mad about dogs as in later life, was the ring-leader, I'm sure, in combining a love of sports statistics and cats. Once, when Snowball had five kittens, when they were of frisking age we decided, somewhat incongruously, to give them old-time boxers' names—John L. Sullivan, Jim Jeffries, etc.—and kept statistics on their wrestling (I know, I know) triumphs: whichever kitten pinned another's shoulders down and kept it there for a count of three won that match.

Larry, Glynn, and cats at the home of Sally Long, Mama's cousin.

Larry succeeded in fostering a pet cat, the only one, that Daddy loved: Tee-Hee (Larry was outrageous in cat-naming) would jump up on Daddy, chew on his buttons, and sashay across his shoulders while Daddy smiled complaisantly. Larry always liked animals better than many human beings.

Later, William Monroe classmates, from the sixth grade on, marveled at his knowing the statistics for any baseball player they could name. Since Daddy did not like or follow football or other sports than baseball, Larry went over to Uncle Ernest's to watch football or other sports on television with him. We didn't have a television anyway. We were certainly separable then, for baseball was the only sport I cared a rap about, and that care has attenuated every year since high school.

Perhaps it was unfortunate that I caught up with Larry in school and he had to suffer invidious comparisons. But I don't think he ever cared then. He would happily settle for a middle station, probably just above the literal middle of his high school classes. Mrs. Stephens would occasionally say something to me like "Baby Brother is original; he did some things that nobody else did on that last assignment," which was commentary on a political cartoon from the newspaper. Like several of our siblings, Larry could do but did not especially want to.

A common image in my head is of the subteen Larry lying across three kitchen chairs, for he was sick a great deal more than I was when we were children. When well, he was usually more active than I ever was. He was mad about games as well as about sports. He was the one who devised cow pasture golf, sinking tuna cans for holes and using putters for all of the driving on the short holes in the cow pasture. He organized the nieces and nephews, calling themselves Jack Nicklaus or Arnold Palmer (really "Almer Palmer" playfully). He played football with them in the front yard. The two of us played an occasional bit of lackluster tennis on the red clay across the road; and we took great long bicycle rides together, though he couldn't keep up with me, and I was not the nicest of bicycling companions.

Larry at about 19, in Baltimore.

In later years, after my college teaching year was ended and wild strawberries were ripe, I would go home for a couple of weeks and Larry would take vacation time from his job as postal clerk to go at the same time. At night he was the chief organizer of the nieces and nephews in all sorts of card cames, using matchsticks or corn or beans in the gambling games, to appease Mama. Also very fond of horse racing and betting the Kentucky Derby, Larry became rather proficient at betting the Derby, perhaps—I don't really know—winning more money than he lost on that one race. Let's leave him savoring his winnings.

I will not attempt any further portrait of myself here, for the whole of this work is about my memories. The clever reader (and all of my readers are clever) will be able to see me in every interstice.

Mama, Larry, and Glynn on our shared tricycle, in the front yard, 1948.

The lives of the members of my immediate family were often not very successful in worldly terms. Technically speaking, most of their lives did not reach the heights of tragedy, though there was certainly often pathos and tragic notes along with the divine comedy. I want to be brisk and not maudlin in this account of the central family that is so much part of my life. But, truth be known, I am crying so that I can hardly see the keyboard right now as I write. My last living sibling, Larry, is desperately ill, and I think back on all of the others and on my parents. Their lives might have been so much better. Except for me, no one in the family was educated up to the level of their intelligence. I know that education does not guarantee happiness; but it could have made a great difference for many of them. It wasn't to be.

Chapter 5

Family: Stage Left and Stage Right

Apart from the family that I lived with all of the time, there are others: in the older and contemporary line, grandparents, aunts, uncles, and numerous cousins. Many people of my time and region had grandparents or even great-grandparents living in their home. I did not. As far as I know, the last of my great-grandparents, my mother's maternal grandmother, died before I was three, and she did not live with us.

The wedding picture of my grandparents, John Ira Baugher and Cora James Lamb, 1892.

Of my four grandparents, one, my father's father, John Ira Baugher, the postmaster, died before I was born. Grandma Baugher, who lived with Aunt Lucille in Baltimore, died when I was nine, so I didn't know her nearly so well as a number of my siblings and cousins knew her. I saw her not so many times in my boyhood, often in the company of Great Aunt Sadie, her sister. I saw Aunt Sadie a bit more often and liked both of them. Grandma was a very short woman, her husband being almost as tall sitting down as she was standing beside him in their wedding picture. When I knew her, she wore standard-issue grandma togs for the time: sober, dark-colored dresses, sometimes with white collars; stack heels; and frequently hats. Her hair was gray or graying from my first remembered encounter, done up in a bun. She seemed to have a lively sense of humor and laughed as much as the rest of us when a fly flew up her nose and came out on the top of her false teeth's upper plate—or was it the other way around?

Great-Aunt Sadie, in Dahlgren, Virginia in 1953.

I knew her as much from others' memories as from my own encounters. Of course, the homeplace had been hers long before it was ours, and she had a lot of play in my mother's memories, more than I ever heard from my father. She was forward-thinking enough to have a telephone, which the household never had in my life there. Mama reports that she liked listening in on the party line. Her greatest moment of triumph was hearing Bea (or was it "Bee"?) Davis speak of getting her foster child, Aunt Ruby, off her hands, when she married Uncle Ernest, Grandma's eldest: "Thank goodness, that problem is off my hands!" Bea told one of her friends. Grandma broke into the conversation, "And into the hands of someone else!" Aunt Ruby, as we'll see later, was quite a case, as we expressed it.

Grandma Baugher appeared to me to be a jolly, good-natured woman. How she could be is a mystery to my grown-up mind. She gave birth to fourteen children, only seven of whom survived to adulthood. One lived to the age of 3. The other six, including her firstborn, were either dead at birth or soon thereafter. She gave birth to children from 1893, when she was 18, to 1919, when she was almost 44. Her oldest living child, Uncle Ernest, was 24 years older than her youngest, Aunt Lucille. How can such a life of losing so many children be borne? How can one thrive? Study history as we might, we are a world apart from earlier days.

Grandma Baugher with Hazel and Joe, Baltimore, 1947.

Granddaddy Baugher was buried at Mt. Paran Methodist Church cemetery, a few miles from the homeplace. When Grandma Baugher died in Baltimore, at age 77, her three daughters, all of whom lived there, wanted her buried there. Three of the four sons lived in Virginia and were perhaps not forthcoming with the money to return her body to Virginia. Mama was scandalized by the couple's being split up that way after death.

My McDaniel grandparents when young, probably in 1908; my mother as a teething baby, chewing on the photographer's comb, and her older sister, Bonnie.

Granddaddy McDaniel, my mother's father, has left me with fewer warm memories than Grandma Baugher. He died at the age of 72 when I was 11; I well remember him, seeing him fairly often. He and Granny Anna (Anna Leah Cox McDaniel) lived with their youngest, Uncle Jinks, 15 years younger than Mama and at the time the only unmarried one of the six children. Though I think that Mildred and Patricia, who saw the McDaniel grandparents more than I did, have some fond memories of Granddaddy McDaniel, I have essentially none. He was an ill-tempered old man when I knew him, hacking and coughing and smoking Camels non-stop. He treated Granny Anna badly, perhaps because, at least according to Daddy, she had been unfaithful to him in their youth. My cousin Myrle

Harlow said that she had seen Granddaddy drag Grandma around the room by her hair.

Mama, always generous about family failings, was devoted to him, remembering how good he was at growing fruit trees, at grubbing up new ground, at growing strawberries, at playing "Soldier's Joy" on his banjo. I experienced none of this firsthand; I saw no affection coming from him, and consequently I had none for him.

My sisters, June and Kay especially, loved visiting Granny Anna, but she was more than a little dotty when I knew her and did not loom large in my childhood. She seemed to have obsessive-compulsive disorder to some extent, never throwing away a newspaper or an eggshell. The new but unfinished house that Uncle Jinks had built was mostly a mess. When she came visiting she usually wore a headscarf and a heavy coat, even in midsummer. Mama always said, "Mama's mind is bad; just overlook it."

That Granny Anna had been a great beauty is evident from the few pictures of her in her youth. According to Mama, people used to say that she was the prettiest woman who ever set foot in Swift Run Baptist Church. According to Daddy, she was chased after by all of the hot bloods around. When my parents, early on, lived with Granddaddy Mac and Granny Anna, according to Daddy, Walter would sprinkle flour on the windowsills to try to catch Anna "stealing a leap," in the quaint parlance of John Aubrey.

I know about none of this firsthand. But Daddy never was cautious about what big-eared little pitchers might overhear, and I, little historian that I was, overheard a lot. In my childhood, Granny Anna was somewhat pitiable: one could see that she had once been a beauty but was now toothless and rather haggard; she seemed smart and better-educated than Mama, but she was driven to expend that little bit in writing pamphlets with titles like "The Wages of Sin," well-written in its way, I judged; she tried to give these pamphlets to people exiting churches who reluctantly took the offering, sometimes.

Mama spoke fondly of how good a cook her mother had been, and I can believe it. However, when we went to visit, she opened cans of Franco-American "spaghetti" and pork and beans. She had given up.

My impression then and now was that she was livelier and more into the world once her cantankerous husband died. She prided herself on naming rock and roll singers that she saw on television when living at Aunt Lizzie's, though she always called Elvis "Evlis Presley," so must have garnered his name from print. She was much more interested in me when I went to college than when I was a little boy, always glad to see me and talk my ear off. And she talked incessantly. I cannot remember much of anything she ever said, but it was clear that she was good-natured and wanted to be liked. Once, still vain without due cause, she said to Mae, my wife, "I'm 75 years old. I don't think I look 75; do you?" Mae kept in reserve what she thought, "No, you look 95." She lived to be 85 and lives on in family catch phrases, though unfortunately most are not flattering: "Oh, don't be as slow-moving as Old Granny Anna!"

Granny Anna at Aunt Lizzie's home in the middle part of her older age.

I wish I knew more of her background—of why her father had the elegant name of Montressa Orient Cox (Where did THAT come from?); of why she gave her children such exotic, wide-ranging names: my mother,

Olga Nethersole McDaniel, named after a famous English stage actress who toured America several times, appearing in one play (*Sapho*) for which she was arrested and tried for public indecency; Fern Norvelle McDaniel; Christopher Columbus McDaniel; Jinks Arlington McDaniel (all right, "Jinks" was his father's middle name [why in the world did the McDaniels name a pair of twins Walter Jinks and Willie Finks {I need an interrobang here}]); of why she was so interested in my going to college when it was not in her family tradition at all, I assume.

I was, on the whole, much closer to some uncles and aunts than to my grandparents. The oldest and chiefest of these is Uncle Ernest, my father's elder brother who lived just across the hill on an adjacent farm, whom I saw just about every day of my youth. Uncle Ernest and Aunt Ruby's children, five of them—Ernestine, Harry, Ray, Frances, and Aubrey—were all essentially a generation older than I was, most of them older than my oldest two sisters; and they were long gone from home, out in the world working, all of them living in Baltimore except Ernestine, who lived in Warrenton, Virginia. Consequently, my family was almost a second family to Uncle Ernest and Aunt Ruby.

They walked from their place to ours (Uncle Ernest's boyhood home) to get the mail six days a week, at least one of them, sometimes both. Since they lived off the road, their mailbox was distant, next to ours rather than down the road at their outlet. Their house was not visible from ours, many hundreds of yards away over the hill. For a period when I was a young boy, Uncle Ernest and Aunt Ruby came over every summer evening after supper and sat talking with Mama and Daddy, the men's chairs leaning back against the front of our house, until it started dusking down dark. We children played around in the front yard as they talked, noting crazy drivers like Razz Shifflett and Lewis Marshall, going like 60 when 60 was something, speeding on the dusty gravel road out front. Uncle Ernest took more interest in cars than Daddy, though, as far as I know, he never drove at all. He knew Henry Js and Kaisers and Frazers, and Willyses and Hudsons, all of which post-World War cars occasionally drove by, and he and Aubrey knew every car that George Marshall, Lewis's father and owner of the general store a little over a mile away, ever owned. As dusk drew down, we chased lightning bugs, the murmur of country gossip as background noise, some of which I hearkened to, never sure just why. And whippoorwills sang plaintively in the trees up at Celt Elementary School.

Uncle Ernest (in the hat) and Daddy in front of our home, 1962.

All of us kids walked over to Uncle Ernest's place, stopping to climb the huge sycamore along the road through the field, almost every day. We kept a weather eye out to see whether his "baggy bull" (We rarely spoke just of the bull.) was around, whether he was pawing the ground and in a sporting mood. (Larry's lament lived in infamy: "Bull gonna get me; bull gonna get me!") We went, not just for the company, but to read the Washington newspaper, the comics especially, look at the puzzles, note Herblock's editorial cartoon, and help Uncle Ernest on the crossword puzzle. When we—Kay, Larry, and I anyway—were still young, Uncle Ernest got a television set. With lots of pipe-wrench turning of the outdoor antenna and fussing with the vertical hold, we saw the wonders of two television stations, Harrisonburg's WSVA, across the Blue Ridge Mountains, about 40 miles away, and Richmond's WTVR, about 75 miles away.

I'm not sure when the television age began for me, probably somewhere between 1952 and 1954; but apparently I was too old for standard children's TV. I disliked every "children's" television program, especially *Howdy*

Doody, but enjoyed night-time comedy like the Colgate Comedy Hour and, when in high school, reveled in sophisticated westerns like *Maverick* and *Sugarfoot*.

With the advent of television, we must have worn out our welcome at Uncle Ernest's, but he and Aunt Ruby generally seemed glad of the company. She would get us to carry in a couple of buckets of water from their spring down a very steep hill, fetch in another box of wood chips from the wood pile and stow with the thirty others in the backroom of their house, for starting fires. Once the chores were done, Aunt Ruby would say "You can turn on. . . and later on in life you can turn out." She affected a kind of sophisticated twist on phrasing to show how worldly she was: ice cream was always just "cream," and cars were always just "machines" ("I heard his machine coming over the hill."), and she rarely used the word "television," saying just "You can turn on." Every now and then she would give us a nickel.

Our pleasures there BTV (before television) were satisfyingly elemental: in the late 1940s Uncle Ernest knew the names of some of the kinds of planes that flew over. Larry and I, at home, would eye a plane and say, "It looks like a P-38 bomber." Occasionally we would see a dirigible or zeppelin, and Uncle Ernest seemed informed. His politics were to the left of Daddy's: he didn't curse FDR and seemed to like Harry Truman. I once heard him say "If I had known there would ever be such a thing as Social Security, I would have lived differently." He and Aunt Ruby had always been rather scrimping and saving; they found it hard to give up the habit when they could have, and he still worked much harder and farmed to a much larger extent than necessary.

I remember his going out on a cold winter night to look after 16 new-born piglets or on a hot summer day going down to his flat—bottomland along the creek—to get in field corn for his cattle, driving Maud and Nell pulling the wagon, down the rumble-rock road, with me holding on to the pole-chain brake on the wagon to keep it from rolling too fast. He had a mule too, Jack I think his name was. He often raised his own wheat and milked many more cows than we did, separating the milk and cream in a centrifugal separator after milking the cows in the lot that they called a cuppen. Mama and Daddy never used the term, which I realized only decades later must have been an elision of "cowpen" and must have come from Aunt Ruby's background.

Except for milking cows, I don't remember Aunt Ruby's working very hard in the years that I knew her. She often didn't cook. They often ate just sandwiches on store-bought bread for supper. Once when Uncle Ernest was at our house in the late afternoon I remember Mama's saying, "Well, I've got to go make some cornbread." Uncle Ernest said, "I don't know when was the last time I had cornbread." We had to try to dissuade Mama from sending him some, sure he would be embarrassed beyond recall.

However, once Uncle Ernest and Aunt Ruby had fenced in their yard to keep the cows out, since they lived essentially in the middle of a large cow pasture, Aunt Ruby delighted in digging up maple saplings and other wild plants and ordering flowers, planting the yard to a fare-thee-well. She went to the woods of Whitelaw Snow's land across the border fence to get stone to pave muddy paths. So she worked hard in a way, saying that she liked "men's work" better. They hired the neighborhood colored woman (so-called at the time), Julia Steppe, to do their wash.

Uncle Ernest seemed glad to have an audience for his jokes, and he WAS funnier than Daddy, but most of his stuff was cornball and often country obscene. On a cold day when we left he was sure to say, "Be sure to put a chip over your ass [or, occasionally softening it, 'tater patch'] tonight so that you don't catch cold." If we saw dancers like the June Taylor Dancers on Jackie Gleason, he would say, "Look, look, you can see punkin busters" (or "funny dusters"), his words for female genitalia. He embarrassed Larry and me, but we tolerated it without encouraging it. He was an inveterate nick-namer. Early on Kay was "Lard-Ass," as noted; later she and June were "Kate and Dupli.CATE"; I was Pete and Larry Repeat; Roy was Stump. And Mama had given most of us one-syllable names because she hated nicknames.

Uncle Ernest always treated me (as did cousin Aubrey) as if he thought me the brainiest person he knew, asking me questions about things sometimes beyond my ken. Of course, I tried living up to his idea of me. I was glad to help him out some on crossword puzzles. He whispered audibly as he read the newspaper and would occasionally cuss a streak or two at what he read. But he was much more gentle-tempered than Daddy, fiercely private about his family matters, much more than Aunt Ruby, always giving things away with her slanted way of talking.

Aunt Ruby seemed to be in awe of Uncle Ernest's mind and abilities. She was a poor strange critter, to adopt the phrasing of my region. Either an orphan or an abandoned child, I don't know which, she grew up as Ruby Newton in higher social circumstances than the Baughers, under the foster care of Bea and Boss Davis, that is, the unmarried Isaaetta Davis and her unmarried brother George W., siblings of Fannie Davis Early, large land-owners a few miles away, what they themselves probably thought of as landed gentry. On the 1910 federal census, Ruby Newton is listed as "adopted" into the household. I don't know how loosely the term was used. Whenever Mama spoke of Isaaetta Davis, her tone always suggested that the woman thought of herself as if she were the Grand Duchess of Cornwall. Ruby was a wild and apparently pretty young thing, riding horses bareback, a tomboyish heller, whom Uncle Ernest laughed at as a young man, the classic prelude to romance in books.

We kids mostly found her genuinely likable, but it must be admitted that she had a snide, sneaky manner of saying things about people, especially Mama, that she considered her social inferiors. She sneered at Alberta Shifflett as the lowest of the neighborhood. I often wanted to tell her that, yes, Alberta was an accomplished liar but better company, without Aunt Ruby's mean streak. Uncle Ernest liked to remind people that we Baughers were distantly related to Alberta. If Aunt Ruby saw Mama scraping new potatoes, the way that we liked them, cooked with some of the wispy peel still on, she'd say, "WE can afford to peel our potatoes."

Perhaps Aunt Ruby's mind had been affected by her epilepsy and the numerous falls she had. It was scary to see her have a seizure, which she had fairly often, once burning her arm in a long stretch by falling on a wood stove. These were called "spells"; she usually had them sitting down. She would black out for a while and come to gradually, rubbing her hand along her thigh all the while, take her pills, and be all right for a number of days. When she said something unusually snarky and condescending to Mama, Mama said, "I just ignore her; her mind is bad." That was Mama's usual explanation of bad behavior.

I remember two occasions that will stand for many, of Uncle Ernest and her children, especially Aubrey, the youngest, treating her badly, which made us pity her although she was often just infuriating. I was unfortunately there when Aubrey was getting ready to return to Baltimore once. I was trapped reading the newspaper, not knowing that an argument overflowed into the room where I was, when Aubrey tore into his mother, saying some of the roughest, most insulting things I've ever heard a son say to his mother. Once Aubrey was gone, I thought Aunt Ruby would be broken up, starting out a sentence, "I never thought I'd live to see the day . . . ." I thought she'd lament being talked to that way, but—in typical Uncle Ernest/Aunt Ruby fashion—she said nothing negative about family. She finished her sentence ". . . that I had a son as handsome as Aubrey."

Another time when Aubrey lived at home for a fairly long period of his adulthood (Mama's theory was that he had gambling debts and fled Baltimore for safety), several neighborhood children were playing there in the front yard while Uncle Ernest, Aunt Ruby, and Aubrey sat on the porch. The two men were chaffing all the children, making lame jokes and having a good time. Aunt Ruby joined in, with a remark not unlike those of her menfolk. At once, Uncle Ernest and Aubrey yelled out in unison "Shut up, Ruby!/Shut up, Mama!" One had to feel sorry for her.

When Aubrey was there for a good while as Larry and I were approaching and in our early teens, he was great fun. At Uncle Ernest's house he taught us to play blackjack and several kinds of poker and pinochle. During the winter he came over to our house to play cards or word games with Daddy, Larry, and me. Especially we played set-back, the Baugher family game par excellence. Larry and I were always partners. Aubrey had the misfortune of always having to partner Daddy, a wild bidder, always opining that an ace and a jack were good for a bid of 4 at least, setting them more often than not and then shooting the moon (and missing). In addition Daddy was a table-thumper as he slapped down his cards, often murmuring phrases like "Don't talk back," which he had overheard as Larry and I listened to rock and roll on the radio from 1956 on. We beat our two elders most of the time, and I won nearly all of the word-games we played, but everyone had a good time. In my youth, all Baughers were game-playing maniacs. Such games were the only game in the non-town, other than sitting at the radio, which we fought over controlling, calling dibs for the night any time after noon.

We liked all five children of Uncle Ernest and Aunt Ruby, much older than Kay, Larry, and I. Aubrey, the youngest, was the most fun and seemed to be the shrewdest (his favorite word); but I saw so much more of him. Ray seemed to be the sweetest-natured, and his step-children, from Glenna's first marriage—Darlene and Darryl—were near our age. It was a delight to see Darryl bouncing a ball on Uncle Ernest's chicken house when a bumblebee, irritated by the banging, followed the ball to the source. Caterwauling ensued. Ray and Glenna's two children together, Danny and Chucky, were a few years younger than Larry and me, young enough to be smiled at indulgently when they sang about Colgate Devil Cream toothpaste. Mama and Daddy especially liked Glenna. All of Ray's family seemed to make a point of coming over to see us when in from Baltimore.

For me, Harry was more problematic: he once compared me to Boll Weaver (of whom, more anon) when I got into a slight fight with his son Jerry. And Selena Detamore Baugher, his wife, always chased Larry and me, trying to kiss us, with Harry helping. Still, he drove Daddy, Larry, and me to see Willie Mays play in a baseball game when he appeared in Charlottesville—a highlight for any baseball-loving boy of that day. From the back seat Larry and I observed what Daddy did not: Harry was going 80 miles per hour on Rt. 29 as he drove us back home in his Pontiac, one of his constant stream of Pontiacs.

Frances was the wise-crackingest of this set of cousins, and she could crack chewing gum better than any other person I ever knew. Her husband, Jim Collins, from the mountains of West Virginia, we liked also, though I'm not sure that Uncle Ernest did. Ernestine, the oldest, we liked; but her husband, the seemingly much older Jesse Courtney, was a rather prickly sort who didn't seem to like anyone much.

Daddy's next brother, Uncle Dave, I scarcely knew, seeing him only twice, I think, in my life. I was surprised when I saw him with his second wife, Margaret: Uncle Dave was a man with a crewcut, looking a deal more citified and business-like than all of the rest. Margaret was driving their car, I think, and cousin Leon says that he never drove. I think that he had two daughters and a son by his now-dead first wife, none of whom I ever met. One, Ruth Baugher Miller, was later to do a lot of the spade work (some inaccurate) on tracing the Baughers back to the 18th-century Lutheran emigre minister Johan Georg Bäger.

Uncle Sidney lived in Charlottesville, about 20 miles away, and we saw him often. He and his wife, the former Dorothy Bickers, had no children. Sid was likable as could be, kind and gentle to his mentally ill wife. She was usually trying her hand at something like writing country music songs, with no success. She sat inside always with a head scarf on and shook her head and said, "It's a sad world" to almost every remark, whether directed her way or not.

Aunt Addie was little known to Larry and me in our youth. Not knowing who she was, we once ran to the woods when she drove in; one of her daughters was driving a big Cadillac whose power steering belt was shrieking as they turned into the driveway. Her son, Eddie Estes, was a great pal of my sisters Hazel and Violet and of Joe, going on trips with Hazel and Joe, but on the whole I didn't know this set of cousins, just the youngest, Susan, indirectly, through her interest in family history.

When I was a teenager, Aunt Addie came to visit for several weeks alone. She helped Mama a great deal around the house, and she and Daddy seemed to have a good deal in common. She organized Mama's kitchen much better than Mama ever did, but I could have told her it was futile: Mama was not well-organized or rational in the kitchen arrangements, but she could really handle things by muddling on in her own way.

Aunt Dolly was a great favorite, picker of huckleberries and blackberries, a warm and comfortable sort of woman married to Armon Walton, something of a drunk. Our three cousins Jimmy, Gretchel, and Maxine (Macky) Walton were friends of my older brothers and sisters. Outside the time limits of this memoir but irresistible as an etching of Aunt Dolly: When she was in her mid-90s (the longest-lived of aunts and uncles), she arose from a sofa to speak to my brother Carl. Her daughter thrust a walker at her, and she responded, "Get that damn thing out of my way!" My kind of elder.

Aunt Lucille, 22 years younger than Daddy, married Odell Sprouse and lived at the homestead for a short while with Grandma Baugher, in 1940 a widow. Then Grandma moved to Baltimore and lived with them. Odell was probably gone by the time that I remember Leon and Nancy Sprouse's coming to Virginia to visit with their mom, Aunt Lucille. They liked visiting there, for Daddy was close, having lived with his mother and Lucille's family while he worked in shipbuilding in Baltimore during World War II. Leon and Nancy were near the age of Larry and me, and we enjoyed their visits. Pretty little Nancy and convivial Leon would sit at the corner of the house eating heavily salted tomatoes and cucumbers, bushels of which Daddy had fresh-picked from his garden. And watermelon feasts followed. Aunt Lucille would pick up from where I left off singing "26 Miles" as she overheard me, her singing voice worse even than mine.

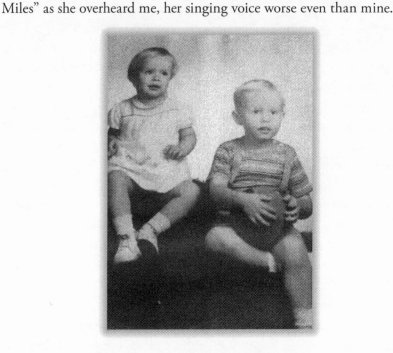

First cousins Leon and Nancy Sprouse, Aunt Lucille's two children.

In 1956, Leon came to stay for a month or six weeks in the summer. I remember Aunt Lucille's parting words: "Fatten him up," and Leon did his part, tucking into the corn-on-the-cob that we had each day. He taught us rummy card games, slightly risqué songs, and all about bikinis. He bragged about having seen the Edsel before it was shown to the general public, and he was mad about the new Baltimore Orioles, talking much about Gus Triandos, pronouncing the –an- syllable in true Bawlmerese, Tree.ENNN. dos. We fought some, almost as if brothers; he would lock himself in his room (the only locking room in the house), and Larry and I crept through the attic to look down into the room sniggering at him.

ii

On Mama's side of the family, we were the closest to the older of her two brothers, Christopher Columbus McDaniel, whom Daddy called Columbus and everyone else called Brother Mac. His wife was named Eleanor, but everyone called her Sis. Three daughters—Mildred, Patricia, and Brenda— were our closest cousins both physically, four or five miles away, living at Mama's old homeplace, and emotionally. We saw each other at least every few weeks, more often in the summer. We would often walk that distance to visit, and Brother Mac would drive us home if he could, if only on a tractor. The four of us, Brenda being too young to always be included, were pretty close in age and the absolute best pals. Mildred Rose was six months older than I was, and Kay cried and cried when Mama would not name me "Melva Rose," the prettiest name she ever heard. Every kind of game that we ever played we played with them, especially set-back, Rook, and several kinds of rummy in the winter, eating whole jars of simple canned beets with salt as we played, and tucking into Mama's homemade cakes with home-canned peaches. In the summertime, hide and seek, played until well after dark, was the favorite. They understood Larry and me as no other childhood friends ever did. They knew all of our shyness and little secrets and would help us get away from surprise visits by strangers if they were there.

First cousins the McDaniel girls: from the right, Mildred, Patricia, and Brenda.

They helped us frighten ourselves when John Glass, the demented grown son of Daddy's sawmill operator, would draw his finger across his throat to indicate that he was going to slit our throats if he ever got the chance.

They taught us euphemistic dirty words like "doo-doo" and "hen-cacky" for chicken poop, filling a gap in our dirty-word vocabulary.

Whenever I think on the delights of childhood games—of long card and board games in winter and helter-skelter running games in summer against a backlit sky full of lightning bugs—it is with Mildred and Patricia, the best set of girl buds that a pair of country boys could ever have. Long, long may they wave.

Sis, who had loved talking with Daddy, especially swapping ghost stories, died in her thirties of a heart condition easily fixed today. Later Brother Mac remarried and had a large family of all boys but one, whom I scarcely know, these next-generation cousins.

Next closest to our family as a whole was the Harlow clan, eight children of Mama's older sister, Aunt Bonnie. Aunt Bonnie, as the country expression has it, could make a dog laugh, and her daughters laughed a lot also. The two oldest daughters, Ethel and Daisy, visited often by themselves, Daisy driving the latest Raymond Loewy-designed Studebaker or a wood-panel station wagon. She was always quite free about letting Larry and me play in her cars, not at all fussy like lots of the adults we knew. When the older daughters left, the Baughers always argued about who was the prettiest of the lot, Daddy plumping for Ethel, but she had red hair, which just didn't cut it with us kids. Mama thought Daisy the prettiest, with wonderful bone structure. We younger ones preferred Myrle, my sister June's best bud. Rachel and Gloria, the two youngest, close to Larry and me in age, we were never especially close to. Gloria was terribly spoiled by her father, Warren Harlow, his little "Ben," but quite nice years later.

First cousin Daisy Harlow, Aunt Bonnie's daughter, on the right, with Hazel
on the steps of her Fleetwood Avenue, Baltimore, apartment, 1950.

The Harlow males Larry and I did not like so well as others did. Jesse,
the oldest, was pretty much a generation older and mostly outside our ken.
Fred was buddies with Omar and Roy somewhat with Carlton, whom
Larry and I mocked because his favorite expression to us kids was always
a smart-ass "Don't worr' 'bout it."

Daddy liked arguing with Warren Harlow, especially pointing out to
him how the television wrestling that Uncle Warren liked so much was all
fake. Bonnie seemed to be Mama's favorite sister, the two of them being
the first in the family.

Mama, on the right, and Aunt Bonnie as little girls, c. 1912.
Apparently chastised by either the photographer or a parent, Bonnie
looks angry and rebellious; Mama looks ready to cry.

Aunt Elizabeth, Mama's youngest sister, had three children—William, always called Bill, shy and likable, with something of a speech impediment that made him shyer; Warner, very smart when young, Roy's close bud; and Juanita, always called Nita, deaf and hard to communicate with. I was not willing to learn sign language, seeing her rather seldom. Mildred and Patricia I think did learn it for her. Aunt Lizzie was easy to like, always in a flurry, she and her husband, Kyle Wood, a cousin, raising thousands of chickens. However, their home was the most boring-ass place Larry and I ever visited, with nothing to do but hop down the concrete sidewalk and listen to the click of the electric fence, or watch stupid day-time television. We had fun with Aunt Lizzie's pronunciation of some words: "Now you shirren [children] be sure to sit down on the back of that truck." She always watched people's faces, eyes and mouth especially, intently when talking to them. Once, she broke in to say, mid-sentence, about me, "Doesn't he have pretty teeth?"

Mama's other sister, Aunt Fern, I never saw in my youth and saw only once, I think, ever in my life. She and Mama were not on speaking terms when I was young. For Mama, whom Daddy always accused of ancestor and family worship, not to speak to a sister, the offense must have been grave. Mama never talked about it that I heard, so I figured that the offense might have had something to do with Aunt Fern's making a play for Daddy. I have no evidence beyond Mama's behavior and her later referring to Fern as if she considered her "no better than she should be," in the quaint 18th-century way of speaking of loose women. One much older daughter of Aunt Fern, Janet Akers, I saw a time or two in my youth.

Mama's youngest sibling, Uncle Jinks, was fifteen years younger than she was, just a few years older than my two oldest sisters. He delighted in trying to teach all of us how to ride a bicycle by sitting on the handlebars facing backward, peddling backwards, so the bike would go forward. A very skilled carpenter, he built our big new barn, a custom kitchen cabinet for mama, and wooden-framed screens for our downstairs windows. He was a conscientious objector in World War II, and even Daddy approved and did not suspect his religion of being bogus. Uncle Jinks married Olgene Snow when he was well past the age of thirty, nearing forty, and fathered two children, but I was grown then and really do not know these cousins.

It's a cliche to say that you can't choose family, but some of mine I would have been glad to choose. Others are distant, mostly because of age differences or geographical distance. Still, most of them were clustered in Greene County, Virginia, and Baltimore, Maryland. Sometimes the Baltimoreans considered "back home" almost heaven. Most often the steadfast Greene Countians and the long-adapted Baltimoreans considered the other place the ass-end of the world.

Chapter 6

Jarfy

When I was a schoolboy at Celt Elementary, geography loomed large in the curriculum. Most of it was world geography, somewhat less national, very little regional, and almost none strictly local. We knew more about Omoo the South Sea Islander than about the Native Americans that once trod where we now walked.

"Jee.OG.ra.fee" seemed to be a much more punctilious pronunciation than we were used to, too prissy for us to respect, so we usually called the subject "jarfy," as in "I still haven't done my jarfy homework." Still, we respected the subject, and most of us could find places on the maps we had. Of all the curricular materials provided for our poor little Celt Elementary School, next to chalk and erasers, maps and globes were probably most common.

The native American Indians were featured some in our study, though scarcely enough in proportion to our fascination with them. Most of our interest, to be sure, stemmed from anecdotal lore of our ancestors and then, more and more, from our reading and listening to radio and viewing television and other suspect sources. Comic books provided a good deal of the distortions we knew—for instance, the lesser characters in Red Ryder.

Anyone with a vivid imagination, a relative with high cheekbones, or word-of-mouth family legends claimed kinship with American Indians. We were puzzled and insulted by Miss Towne's countering our boasts of Indian kinship with the prim "That's nothing to be proud of."

Our scholastic knowledge of the Indians, such as it was, came more from our fourth-grade textbook on the history of Virginia than from geography, the history book a thick brownish quarto we marched through and bivouacked in day by day. I can still remember some pictures better than the logorrhea of the text, of hogsheads of tobacco for shipment to England and of the Powhatan Indians' kind of domicile. The Powhatans were the Indian nation encountered at Jamestown, the most powerful of Virginia's eight nations (I use "nation" in the strict geographical sense), and probably the most friendly.

We were surrounded by Indian artifacts, those in Celt apparently of the Monacan nation. The Monacans buried their dead in mounds. On Elijah Durrette's farm in the bottomland on the way over to Brother Mac's there is a mound right in the midst of the flat bottomland. We thought, perhaps correctly, but probably not, that it was an Indian burial mound. Larry and I tried to dig there once, but it was so rocky that we gave it up soon, rationalizing that it was probably better not to desecrate the place anyway. Thomas Jefferson is sometimes called the father of American archaeology because he had no such qualms (and had slave labor). He excavated a well-known Monacan burial mound near Monticello, close to us.

The geography of Celt explained why the artifacts were there in the thousands. After every spring plowing of our main garden, even after at least fifty years of having the same area plowed, we would find arrow heads, perfectly flinted, mostly unbroken still. After very hard rains, long after spring plowing, we would go out to look for arrow heads; we usually found some. We mostly did not find larger implements or tools, but what rich hunting must have been there in Celt! Arrow heads can still be found on the homeplace whenever ground is newly disturbed.

Though I know of no archaeological digs ever done in Celt, it must have been a good place for Indian settlement or encampments as well as hunting, for the whole countryside teems with springs. Such a source of fresh water would be necessary for Indian encampments, whether for hunting or living, as, later, for the division of land into farms on which one could subsist. Rare is the farm in Celt that had to resort to digging or drilling a well, and such farms are mostly quite small, the result of land-splitting over the centuries. Our wonderful spring, source of all of our water, which never ran dry, was just one of at least four springs within a not-so-very-far bucket-toting distance of our house.

Every spring, of course, had a little stream that emanated from it, good for livestock of every kind. Our pigpen was built around an area through which the stream from our spring ran. The cows had ready access to numerous little streams. The human stock of this land, children in particular, relished the streams almost as much as the pigs and cows did. Before air conditioning was common, dabbling in streams was the best way to cool summer's intemperance. Rare is the child who does not delight in mud and wet sand. We stuck our bare feet in wet sand, packed the sand over a foot, carefully withdrew the foot, displaying our cave-like "toad-house," as satisfying as building sand-castles.

These little runlets from springs were always called "branches," never too wide to jump across. Thus the formulaic phrase "whiskey and branch water." Where we lived, somewhat bigger streams were known as "creeks," as in "Quarter Creek," over near Mama's homeplace on the road to Quinque. We knew that one of the borders of Uncle Ernest's rich bottomland farming flat was a nameless-to-us creek that wound down through Whitelaw (pronounced "WHYTE.ler") Snow's flat until it emptied into the river that ran through Elijah Durrette's (We thought Mama was saying "Dirt.") flat. If we walked over to Brother Mac's through the fields rather than the longer way around the roads, we had to ford both Snow's Creek and Durrette's River on the way. There was no hard-and-fast rule, but we knew that it wasn't a "river" until it was more than, say, ten feet wide. The silly old local maps called both Chapman's River and Durrette's River "Swift Run." We recognized the word "crick," as in "Good Lord willing and the crick don't rise," but never used that pronunciation ourselves.

All of this seeming solidity of what to call various-sized streams was knocked awry when we visited Daddy's Aunt Sadie and her family in Dahlgren, Virginia, and Daddy's first cousin once removed, Jollett Steppe, took us out in a motorboat on a huge body of water called Machodoc Creek. It seemed like these Navy people didn't know English very well.

Greene County has far fewer actual rivers than creeks, branches, and runs. We called a river what is called a "run" on official maps—for example, "Elijah Durrette's River" instead of "Swift Run," though the church, Mama's church, nearby but not on the river, was called Swift Run. What maps have as Roach River, we called "Ed Collier's," as in "I'm going fishing down at Ed Collier's bridge" or "Early's River," named for Ed Early, the husband of Fannie Davis Early, whose large land holdings were on that river.

The two largest rivers within our ken in Greene County—the oft-flooding South River, out beyond Stanardsville, and the Rapidan, part of the border between Greene County and Madison County—we always called by their proper names. South River, a good fishing stream, was quite familiar, though it was a bit over seven miles away, a big trip for us.

Greene County, as far as I knew, had no lakes. Now it has a number of man-made lakes for realty development. Farm ponds were scarce in my youth but are now very numerous indeed, sometimes with good fishing.

As much in our eyes in Celt as the streams at our feet were the mountains, the glorious, gorgeous Blue Ridge Mountains, the closest less than four miles from Celt, the ones behind which the sun set no more than eight miles away as the crow flies. The whole northwestern boundary of Greene County is made up of the Blue Ridge Mountains, the county line being essentially the Skyline Drive along the peaks in the Shenandoah National Park.

I can remember a suite-mate of mine in graduate school, one from the flat land of Ponca City, Oklahoma, querying in wonder, "You have part of a NATIONAL park in your home county?" Yes, I do. Part of the mountain land was evacuated in the 1930s for the formation of the Shenandoah National Park. The mountain people were nearly all "resettled," an area of Greene County called The Resettlement at the foot of the mountains. Daddy, especially, remembered the bitterness of the mountain folk forced out. Starting in the 1920s, the state of Virginia ceded some of the land of eight counties to the federal government on the condition that it be used for a national park.

If one goes over the mountains on Federal Route 33, which passes through Stanardsville, through the eastern part of the Shenandoah National Park, through Swift Run Gap at the top of the mountain (where then-Lieutenant Governor Alexander Spotswood, in 1716, led his Knights of the Golden Horseshoe to explore western Virginia), across the Skyline Drive and down the mountain in Rockingham County, turning left into

Beldor, a rural community at the very base of the mountain, one is in Baugher terrain. On the left of the road to Beldor, a few hundred yards INSIDE Shenandoah National Park, is the Maiden/Baugher/Hensley Family Cemetery, grandfathered in, the graves not dispossessed of their dead Baughers and others. These are not my direct ancestors but a fraternal line to my great-grandfather Jeremiah McMullen Baugher. Some Baughers were dispossessed of their land to form the national park, but I think not any of my **direct** ancestors.

When I was a boy, the only place other than Monticello my father was willing to take regular day trips, to actually travel to see, was into these mountains, to drive through Shenandoah National Park, on Skyline Drive, at the tippy-top of Greene County, to climb up to Senator Harry Byrd's Hawk's Nest, to descend to Dark Hollow Falls, to visit caverns just outside the park on the other side of the mountains.

Visiting Skyline Drive, in Shenandoah National Park, 1953:
Carl, Glynn, Roy, first cousin Aubrey Baugher, Larry, Kay,
Mama holding her first grandchild (Gail), and Hazel.

Most of the beautiful stonework of the bridges and hardscaping in this park was done by the CCC (Civilian Conservation Corps). Perhaps, had I pushed my father, even he would have admitted that this was something that the loathed FDR did that earned his respect.

Strange to think that these mountains, so close, so much a part of the daily life of our vision, were so selectively known. If I look on a detailed map, I see that the single mountain peak closest to my home is Crow Mountain, only about two miles away. I never heard its name until I looked at a map to write this chapter, and I doubt that we thought of it as a mountain. Right behind it is Parker Mountain, which I heard of constantly. We could not have a cold snap without Mama's saying, "Wrap up! It's going to get cold around Parker's Mountain [She added the possessive.]" A few miles from Parker is Bingham Mountain, a peak I also heard of a great deal. It's up at Dyke, near where my great-grandfather Jeremiah lived, before my time. The next mountain to Bingham is Brokenback, bearing almost the same name as that in Annie Proulx's long short story and the movie. Again, I never heard it mentioned the whole time I was growing up about four miles away. How could this be? I suppose that this bit of geography did not touch our daily life. Yet Flat Top and High Top, right up there in the range at the county's end, I heard named a great deal, perhaps because of their elevation, perhaps because they were on Skyline Drive, perhaps because our local "mountain hoogies" spoke of them often.

In school I learned that these near and familiar mountains, yet strange enough to have black bears (before they made a comeback) and rattlesnakes, were "old worn-down mountains," part of the oldest mountains in all of America. They were so close, yet as blue as mountains usually are at a great distance seen through atmospheric haze. We heard about them in song: "In the Blue Ridge Mountains of Virginia,/ On the trail of the lonesome pine . . . ."

Nearly opposite to these, on the southeast horizon, was one lone mountain, not a range. We called it Fray's Mountain, after the man who ran the all-purpose store at Advance Mills, in Albemarle County, just as we called Advance Mills "Fray's." This mountain, with a blinking light atop, apparently to warn planes from the then-tiny Charlottesville airport, scarcely merited the name, in comparison to the grand sweep of the Blue Ridge viewed from the highest cow-pasture hill behind our house and above the spring.

Often the highest peaks had a bit of snow in winter when we had nothing down at the foot. 'Twasn't fair, of course, but nobody expected the weather to be just, despite kids' wishes.

I learned in school that we lived in the Piedmont section of Virginia, from the Romance languages' "foot of the mountain." The foot, indeed: we could see its toenails. But the mountains were not so close as to block the sun or present an ugly view.

About two-fifths of our land was wooded, with tulip poplar trees in the west, toward the Blue Ridge, being the most evident from the house, soaring straight up, limbless, glowing yellow in the fall of the year. Above our spring was a gigantic poplar, perhaps five feet in diameter and 150 feet tall, and a huge V-shaped maple a few yards away, always ready to split in two. We also had a lot of pines in the westerly direction. When Mama sent us to carry jars of water to Daddy and the older boys cutting wood, she directed us "over in the pines." But the trees were quite mixed, later growth of maple, gum, different kinds of oak, hickory, you name it.

Mama always spoke very fondly of the glorious American chestnut trees that had been killed by the blight, but I don't know whether any of these soaring wonders had been on the homeplace. They had been all up in the mountains, Virginia giants to rival California's, providing beautiful lumber, mast for livestock, and a living for quite a few mountain people. Mama said that they tasted like giant chinquapins, not like the inferior Chinese chestnuts we know today.

One stand of huge oaks, several dozen of them, grew on the hill above our main garden, at the edge of the cow pasture next to the part of Uncle Ernest's woods adjacent to the rutted road to his house. Mama grieved, and Larry and I regretted the loss of a favorite playground, when Daddy sold these oaks for lumber, to make money for some project or other, what I do not remember. I remember the oaks with longing still.

Perhaps three-fifths of our sixty-three acres was cleared land, most of it cow pasture, with no large flat portion to be used for farming on any large scale, no land for wheat fields or huge cornfields for livestock feed-growth. But we had no tractor or even horse team for such tillage. The cow-pasture grass grew tall by summer's end. We called the dried grass broomsage, perhaps knowing that "broomsedge," the literary term used in Virginia's own Ellen Glasgow's novel *Barren Ground*, was more accurate. (Willa Cather was also Virginia-born but didn't seem to write about it, leaving the state when young.) Broomsage, probably a sign of poor land and too few cows, was lovely for children to hide in, to duck down in and rise up just enough to fire our cap pistols at the Indians on the horizon. We burnt the hillside broomsage each spring to allow the growth of new grass and clover, though an occasional Scotch thistle and wild blackberry briar would grow too. I delighted in watching cows wrap their tongues oh so gingerly around young thistle blooms to bite off what seemed to be a taste treat.

At the borderline between geography and natural history lies the study of that which covers the earth. While much of Greene County's soil is reddish, almost every acre of our land was brown and somewhat loamy. In April and beyond, dogwood, redbud, and honeysuckle bloomed. Along abandoned fence lines, sassafras, black walnut, and black gum—tupelo— grew. We chewed both the green leaves and the green twig-bark of the sassafras. If we could find wintergreen bushes, pop! went those twigs into the mouth. On the banks and in the margins of the branches grew mints that we chewed, along with unknowns that we could not browse on.

As we prowled the hills, we noted goldfinches on the thistles and eyed Eastern bluebird nests deep in partly rotten fence posts. In the sour cherry trees at the house, the worse-than-bluejay mockingbirds and catbirds marauded and kept up their ugly chatter. (Harper Lee, either you or your character Miss Maudie—saying that mockingbirds never destroyed anyone's garden— knows next to nothing about mockingbirds despite the excellent title and book!)

Back to geography proper. There was no or almost no industry in Greene County in my youth, if you discount farming and moonshining. Even then I knew that partly this owed to there being no railroads in the county. As far as I know, there never was and now probably never will be. Hindering industrial development in a different way, the mountains covered a fair portion of the very small county, now the sixth-smallest county of Virginia's 95, formed from the westernmost portion of Orange County in 1838 and named for Gen. Nathanael Greene, the leader of the southern army in the American Revolution.

Of course shopkeepers, gas station attendants, feed-store workers (Stanardsville had George Davis's Southern States), and other dealers with the public—such as post office clerks, bankers, and school teachers—found local employment. In Stanardsville, Collier Brothers, their building still on the corner there, was our chief source of the few groceries we bought and other general store necessities like shoes for school. Both of the Collier men and their wives were great favorites: Mama gave a bit of her scant business to Blakey's store and to Violet Moyers, but she was loyal to the Colliers.

Almost every hamlet worthy of a name had a little general store, sometimes combined with a post office. Granddaddy Baugher probably sold a few things in his Celt post office. The general store for Celt, a bit over a mile from our home, was run by George and Carrie Marshall in my day, the first people I knew who had a television set.

A fair amount of pulpwood cutting went on, given the scant human population and large tree acreage. Daddy cut pulpwood from time to time, a few pictures in the late '40s showing that he had a short, powerful truck, larger than a pickup, a dually, apparently for hauling it. This wood Daddy and the older boys cut with bow saws or crosscut saws, a hard scrabble. I scarcely remember that truck and wonder whether Daddy or Fred, about 18 then, drove it. In my memory Daddy usually got Uncle Kyle Wood to haul it to sell in Charlottesville to a Mr. Forbes of Forbes Lumber Company. But employment for pay was not much available in Greene County. So those who sought such employment often went to Charlottesville, twenty miles or more away.

This tendency, increasing over the decades, has made Greene County something of a bedroom community for congested, sprawling little Charlottesville. In 1950, Greene County had a population of 4,745, and this fell still lower by 1960, when I went away to college. The population was lower in 1960 than in 1860. In the census of 2010, Greene County had 18,403 people, about 400% of what it was in my childhood days.

Land had been dirt-cheap decades before. I think that Daddy bought the homeplace—the house, outbuildings, and 63 acres—for $2,000 in the early 1940s. Now some of that same homeplace is selling for between $10,000 and $20,000 **PER ACRE,** even in 7-acre lots.

Had I been a philosophical and historical boy, I might have wondered in the 1950s why Greene County was so poor, unpaved, and backward. In front of my house ran an unpaved gravel or dirt road, not unlike many, perhaps most, secondary roads in the county. Periodically, large yellow roadscrapers went over these roads, scraping out uneven spots, removing mud puddles, cleaning and resculpting the roadside ditches, and shaping the crown of the roadway. When working on Rt. 604 in front of our house, the roadscraper would park on the grounds of Celt Elementary School across the road when day's work was done. Larry and I logged many a late-afternoon ("evening" in our language for anything after noon) hour driving an immobile big machine.

A subject of pride in my youth—how close we lived to historical greatness—might have been a subject for deeper questioning: Why did none of it touch Greene County? About 20 miles from where I lived, at Shadwell in the next county, Thomas Jefferson was born; just a little further away Jefferson's Monticello sat atop a small mountain, where Thomas Jefferson had lived his productive life. About twenty miles away from Celt was the University of Virginia, in little Charlottesville, also the product of Jefferson's design and drive. Just a very few miles from Thomas Jefferson lived James Monroe at Ash Lawn. He and Jefferson could see each other's house through a small telescope. Also twenty-some miles away, in Orange County, which then contained Greene, partly adjacent to Albemarle, sat the home of James and Dolley Madison. So the authors of our Declaration of Independence and Constitution were nearly our neighbors, out of historical sync. About 50 miles away Woodrow Wilson was born and raised, and lived much of his adult life. Scarcely 100 miles away—no distance worth mentioning today—George Washington was born, and also about 100 miles away he later lived at Mount Vernon. All of this greatness and achievement so close, and not that far away in time, and yet it seemed to be a different world from where I lived. The geography was not a great deal different, but they were different worlds.

Greene County had no cities in 1950 and still has none. It had, and has, only one town, the county seat, Stanardsville, if a place with fewer than 1,000 inhabitants, now fewer than 500, can be called a town. The English would call it a village. Ruckersville, at the intersection of federal routes 33 and 29, is a "census-designated place," in the jargon of measuring population, but this second-largest settlement is not a town, even in the American sense of the word.

In my youth names of hamlets and small settlements were numerous, many of them now fading from use, like Celt, along with their post offices. In my day, going "up" the road from Celt, hanging a left at "the New Road," about a half mile from home, traveling about two and a half miles, we could turn left on Rt. 810 and soon come to Dyke, with a name of unknown origin. From Dyke we could drive right up between Brokenback and Slaters Mts. almost to Flat Top and the Shenandoah National Park. Along the way we would pass St. George, Pirkey, and Bacon Hollow, none much bigger than Celt.

Had we turned right on 810, we could drive toward Stanardsville, through March, Haneytown, and Geer. In the northwest quadrant of the county, we could visit Lydia or McMullen. Near Quinque, over at Mama's homeplace just behind Swift Run Baptist Church, was what Daddy called Scuffletown, though the only settlement of that name listed on local maps is in Orange County. Most of these little settlements, out-of-the-way drivers might not know they had driven through. This is quintessential Greene County: Borneo, Mutton Hollow, and Bris (where the Blue Ridge Industrial School is located, at St. George).

Peopling these settlements were mostly families deriving ultimately from England, Scotland, Ireland, and—more rarely—Wales. Names like Lamb (or Lam or Lamm)—my Grandma Baugher's maiden name, Morris, Collier, Gentry, Haney, Price, Miller, Raines, Snow, or Cox—all of them English—pepper the landscape. I chose these common English names because all of them are my ancestors. Most of the Macs in the county came from Ireland, but "Mac" and "Mc" are Scottish patronymics; they were Scotch-Irish, part of the plantation of Scotch Protestants in the north of Ireland. Me mither was a McDaniel. The Irish Irish were in Greene County too, the Fitzhughs, the Dulaneys, the Sullivans. Perhaps the best-known Welsh names are Williams and Jones, but we had Reese also, which I suspect was originally Rhys.

All of the Baughers in the county, and indeed almost certainly all of the Baughers in the United States, were German-descended, the paterfamilias being Johan Georg Bäger, who came as a Lutheran minister to Pennsylvania in 1752. His sons, some of the seven, with the changed name spelling, emigrated to the Shenandoah Valley and beyond, across the mountains to Greene County.

The most common name in Greene County, Shifflett in all of its variant spellings, with any combination of one –f or two, one –t or two, perhaps with an –e on the end, is something of a mystery. I have heard all of my life that the name is apparently German, these people being descendants of the Hessian soldiers hired as mercenaries in the American Revolution. This account presents several problems: There were Shiffletts in the area before the American Revolution; the spelling certainly appears more French than German, with the French ch- of a genuine name, Chifflet, pronounced like an sh- in English, being transmuted; and theories abound, but their very contradictions show the lack of hard evidence. I have at least one Shifflett as an ancestor also, on the Baugher side. Still no one, to my knowledge, has explained why it is the most common name in the area.

In 1950, we had smatterings of other nations' names in the county, but not nearly the whole United Nations of names that can be found today. For good or bad, we were a rather homogeneous lot.

Negroes, the common racial name at that time, constituted around 7% of the county's population. The county had never had plantations, really, or very large farms, so the population of slave-descended people was lower than one might otherwise expect in this Southern state. In Celt I never knew of but four black families—the lone Phil Reeves, who was a chauffeur and other worker for Fannie Early when I was a very small boy; the Steppes, for a time our nearest neighbors up the road; the Blakeys, less than a mile up the road over in a field; and living with the Blakeys, Grant Jackson, a blacksmith who still eked out a living in his 80s. (Born soon after the Civil War, Grant Jackson had a twin brother, Lee.) The Negroes' names, of course, are ultimately derived from whites, so I have no idea where in Africa these people's ancestors originated.

Today most of the whole wonderful crazy quilt of nations that make up the peoples of the United States are probably represented in Greene County. Still, English names are the most dominant in total number, Morris perhaps second in number only to Shifflett.

The homogeneity was evident in religion when I was a boy, as might be expected from the ethnic groups present. As far as I know, no religion other than Christianity was present in my childhood years. Not only did we have no synagogue, let alone a mosque, I'm almost certain there were no Jews in the county in my time, though there had been earlier. There was not even a Catholic church until 1980. So the religious believers were perhaps all Protestant Christians, and just a few sects of those. Since many of the first settlers were English, they were mainly Church of England and thus, after the Revolution, Episcopalians. The Episcopalians early had a number of missions and schools in the mountains, and Grace Episcopal Church survives in Stanardsville. It is a simple white-painted wood country-style church, Carpenter Gothic, but in my youth it was considered high church: it had solid blue windows and kneeling benches.

Methodists, Baptists, Brethren, and Pentecostals made up most of the county, the last of these four being the late-comer and made up mostly of mountain people. At Amicus, about two miles from home, was a Seventh-Day Adventist church since the 1930s, its members worshipping on Saturday, refusing to eat pork, and expecting the new millennium any day. Yettie Walton, about a mile up the road, was the Adventist that we knew best. Latecomers in the mountains in western Greene County, the Mennonites now have a mission at Mission Home.

Mama seemed to consider anyone other than a Baptist to be a little bit deficient in sanctity. Still, perhaps not: her best-loved sister, Bonnie, was of the Church of the Brethren; some of us children, Kay and I mainly, went to Mt. Paran Methodist with Miss Towne; and we went to summer Bible school at the Stanardsville Methodist church. The county didn't even have a Presbyterian church, for Gawd's sake, back in the 1950s.

Rolling hills, lots of small streams and springs, wooded land and cow pasture, almost totally rural, with fine mountains visible everywhere in the county, a part of a national park and the Skyline Drive—this is the topography of Greene County, much of the jarfy there etched in my brain.

Chapter 7

For What Do We Live . . .?

Talking to his daughter Elizabeth, Jane Austen's Mr. Bennet asks, mostly rhetorically, "For what do we live, but to make sport for our neighbours, and laugh at them in turn?" I'm sure that the Baughers made some sport for our neighbors, and we did our share of laughing at them. However, our neighbors mostly lived too far away for the sport to be easily had, from overhearing. Mostly it arose the old-fashioned way—from story-telling and tale-bearing. And more serious reactions arose at least as often.

Our next neighbor down the road, our closest in space, only several hundred yards away, was Alberta Shifflett Shifflett Hunt. Yes, she was a Shifflett who married a Shifflett for her first husband, Bob, and then C. C. Hunt (Clinton) for her second once Bob was dead. Her first husband I never knew, and her second for only a few years before he died. Most of our family seemed to think her first name was "Alverta," and that's what we called her. Mama said that she had been a tiny woman when first married, only 90-some pounds. The woman that we knew was the fattest of all our acquaintances, probably, though Myrtie Bell Hodges, of whom more later, perhaps rivaled her.

Her greatest talent was perhaps lying, not generally malicious or even especially petty. Perhaps she thought that she spoke truth, so effortlessly did she spin her untruths. I found her generally quite likable, perhaps because she seemed to really like us and was good-tempered and a good audience despite her troubles.

Many days she came laboring—toddling with slow waddles—up the road, shod in great big men's work shoes with pieces cut out to give her corns relief. I remember her saying, "Shoes can't be so expensive that I wouldn't take a knife to them to make them comfortable." On her head she often had a man's hat, looking rather like a Bolivian woman with continents confused. Sometimes she wore a homemade bonnet like the little woman on Old Dutch Cleanser, though usually patterned rather than white. (This was the high day of patterned chicken-feed sacks.) Her face and eye-color somewhat resembled the portraits of Samuel Johnson that I saw much later.

Perhaps I never saw her without an apron on, though her dress itself was often soiled. She kept a spotless house, her kitchen stove especially. Mama said it was because she rarely cooked. Perhaps she didn't: Mama, who would have fed a zombie in need ("Po' ole thing"), nearly always gave food to her and her two grown sons who came with her. They never refused.

Alberta had the prettiest flowers around and was always willing to give Mama a "sign" (I suppose, technically, a "scion," but we called it "sign") or a "slip" of whatever she had going, especially of peonies, pronounced in the local way as "pee.OH.nees." A few "Festiva Maxima," the most fragrant peony I know, here at Emory came from LaVale, which came from the homeplace, which derived ultimately from Alberta.

It was something to see her work on her flowers, enough to traumatize any growing boy: she generally did not get down on the ground, such was her heft, but leaned over until one could see way up her blue-veined, milk-crock-sized legs as her dress rode up in back. She claimed to have been struck by lightning, twice, and may have: I've never seen since anybody with such terrible cascades of broken veins and other blood vessels of all sizes.

Alberta had five children by Bob and one by Clinton. Ernest Davis, not the oldest but the most successful, had moved to Baltimore and prospered, becoming the owner of a small fleet of big trucks. When he came home, he was one of Daddy's best buds, bringing Daddy cigars, talking for hours on end. He had been in the Merchant Marines and had lots of tattoos to prove it. He married a swarthy Baltimore-Italian woman. And his brother Herman P. (middle name, Parker) married another one, a relative of the wife of Ern Dave (so Alberta called him affectionately). I had fun imagining the cuisine of these apparently-Sicilian-American women feeding their hillbilly husbands. Indelibly burned on my retina is the image of Alberta sitting in the tiny back seat of Ern Dave's new late-model Thunderbird. How was that engineering feat accomplished?

Herman P. (sometimes familiarly "P.-Parker" to Fred and Carl) was the absolute best bud of my two oldest brothers. He towered above them—a laughing, enthusiastic, peach-picking, hunting, shooting, fishing, skinny-dipping whirlwind. He was probably the one who talked Fred and Carl into going with him (in Fred's truck, I think) across the mountain to Elkton to court girls from Rockingham County. He came back all enthusiasm, saying, "Those Elkton girls are as pretty as doll-babies." But he went to Baltimore when he quit school. It was sad to see him try to visit Fred on trips back to Virginia after the onset of Fred's schizophrenia. They couldn't carry on a conversation anymore.

Alberta's one daughter, Carrie, lived in Charlottesville and was married, her husband's name Sacre (pronounced SAY.cree), but her name to us was always Carrie Coon, I don't why other than for the alliteration. Perhaps it was actually her name. I scarcely knew her but was surprised at how stately and rather pretty she was. Whenever Carrie came home, you may be sure that Alberta cooked. Mama always announced it by saying "I guess Alverta is putting the big pot in the little," a phrase that didn't make literal sense, but we always knew its meaning. (Mama had tons of these strange expressions.)

The two sons that lived at home with Alberta and always came with her were simple and what was generally called "afflicted" in those days. The older of these two, the firstborn in the family, William Ed, elided so that it sounded like "Wilya.MED," could barely walk, using a long stick as a cane. Mama thought that he had been beaten severely by Bob Shifflett, almost crippling him. I don't know, but the difficulty progressed. Earlier he had gone to pick wild strawberries, sprawling on the ground, squashing many, to sell to any who would buy. Sitting in our house, talking and eating Mama's cornbread, he would make a swift move with his hand and apparently catch a fly just as subtly as Barack Obama. My brothers said he ate the flies he caught, but I don't know: perhaps it was just a feint.

His brother, Weaver, named for a doctor, was very able-bodied, often maddening in his untruthfulness, simple-minded in showing off his latest pocket knife, nearly always with gallon lard tins tied to his belt loops in berry season, trying to make some money. He would go to the general store and all over the county, hitching rides, sometimes being driven long distances to be abandoned by country yokels who thought this a good joke. He was maddening the way he showed up whenever we had visitors at home. His nicknames were, naturally, Boll Weaver and, since his full name was Delward Weaver Shifflett, "Devilish Weaver," Roy's preferred epithet.

Alberta's one child by her second husband was Dallas Hunt, a year or two older than Larry, a good-looking, floppy-haired boy, almost blond, who went to school at Celt for a few years and then was taken to Baltimore by Ern Dave, returning "talking proper," in Weaver's words, calling his adopted home "Bawlmer" and speaking of the mayor, which he pronounced "mur," trying to impress me.

A few hundred yards further down the road, on the other side of the dirt road, up on a gulleyed hill, sat the run-down sprawling home of the Marshalls. Jimmy, a year or two older than Larry, and Kenny, in our grade at Celt Elementary, whose mother had left their father, lived with their grandparents—Lily and Tom Marshall—and their great-grandparents— Alfred and Alsee (or some such spelling) Hearn. For a few years Jimmy and Kenny were the best buds that Larry and I had nearby, boys to bicycle with, to walk down to Durrette's River and skip flat stones across the surface, to go exploring and spin yarns about Indians. We made bike trails on the side of the red clay banks by the side of the road near Uncle Ernest's woods.

But Kenny and Jimmy's elders were a problem: Tom Marshall, who came to our house fairly often, was an inveterate tease, in a hateful way. He always walked with a cane, with which he grabbed kids by the ankles, saying, "C'mere, little girl/little boy." Mostly we eluded him. When a bunch of kids played a pickup game of hide and seek at the Marshall home, Lily and her mother, sitting on the front porch, delighted in pointing fingers at where people were hiding. Then what was the point of hiding?

June and Kay liked going down to the Marshalls' home when their relatives Dorothy and Sharon Liskey were visiting, daughters of Freeman and Ida Liskey, from Harrisonburg. Daddy had dated Ida in his youth and called her Ida-Red after the popular song. The four girls would play jangly almost-tunes on the old piano there.

Once we four boys went to Stanardsville to William Monroe, we drifted apart—different classrooms, different friends and interests; Jimmy was mooning after a girl named Cecilia; and the Marshall boys moved to Charlottesville to live with their father.

Most of the other people down the road to the Albemarle County line we knew but didn't have many dealings with. The Conleys seemed almost to speak a private language among themselves, and the older ones were very hard to understand. Reese and Virginia we knew from school but didn't hang with.

Most of the Conleys—Elmer Reese, Ressie, Margaret, Richard, Hoover, Thelma (Elmer Reese, Reese, Ressie—what was with that obsession?)— were much older than Larry and me, though the cousin Virginia, who lived there, and Reese were not. Mr. Conley was so sour-tempered a grump that we didn't go there. I had never seen the house, back off the road.

In later years, after I had gone from Celt, Mrs. Conley—Loney— became one of Mama's staunchest friends, coming to see her nearly every day, her sons Richard and Hoover dropping her off as they drove up to the general store to hang with other lollygagging men after a hard day's work in the fields. Loney was persistent, even when our lone goose, the one in love with one of our dogs, attacked the skirts of her long dress every time she came.

Abe Dulaney was the next down the road, living in a cinder-block house that doubled as a small store. He was the only arch-enemy that Daddy had. I'm not sure what started the animosity, but I remember two items. Daddy informed the authorities so that Abe, our school bus driver at that time, could not spend county money driving his bus back and forth after his morning delivery of students. And Abe had attempted to throw Roy off the bus and let him ride no more because Lutie Shifflett said that he said a dirty word. But I don't think that either of these actions was the cause of the hatred, just the result.

Abe's wife, Delilah (more alliteration—Delilah Dulaney), had left him years ago. Mama said that in part she just couldn't stand Abe's skinflint ways. He wouldn't let her cook but one food at a time, saying the classic line, "When I have beans, I have beans; when I have taters, I have taters." And so the marriage ended, but probably not in divorce.

Jesse James Shifflett (I think that was his real name; my brothers all called him that.) lived a little farther down the road. He tooled along in his pickup at thirty miles per hour and drove to the general store to sit and talk every single day of his life that the store was open. I almost never saw Mrs. Shifflett: she didn't go to gossip at the store like Jesse. The other grown children we knew distantly. An older daughter, I'm pretty sure, was the wife of Brooksie Taylor, the only man I knew in the 1950s who drove a Renault. (Charlottesville had a foreign motors dealer, sponsoring the baseball Game of the Day on radio, with a deranged woman's voice shrilling out each day of Fiats: "They're a BIG name in Europe.")

The only other neighbors down the road that I want to memorialize a bit were William and Shorty Bickers, bachelors both, short and plump, with porcine faces, farmers that lived, always, in bib overalls, living down a rutted road not so far off Rt. 604. They were good-tempered, and apparently Mama and Daddy and Uncle Ernest and Aunt Ruby enjoyed their visits. They had no conversation for small fry. Their sister, always known as Miss Janie, taught the fourth grade for years and years at William Monroe and was married to our sheriff, Wilbur "Hooks" Deane. Still, she was always Miss Janie to her students.

Turning around at the Albemarle County line, less than a mile from the house, going back up the road, passing Alberta's stucco house, we will turn right into the outlet of Uncle Ernest's place and Dan Collier's place. Maybe a hundred yards up the muddy, rutted drive there was a gate so that Uncle Ernest's cows couldn't get out. Just on the other side of the gate a rutted red-clay road branched to the right and after a bit went up a sudden hill and down a bit again to Dan and Lois Collier's.

Earlier, this had been the home of my classmate George Lamb's family, though it was before I reached an age of memory and perhaps before George did too. Now it was the home of Uncle Ernest's farm worker, mule-driver, and chief object of Uncle Ernest's cusses. At a second gate, as one started down the hill to Dan and Lois's, a pen of anywhere from 12 to 20 starveling foxhounds sent forth a baying chorus. Not that Dan rode to hounds; he ran through the woods at night encouraging the dogs by blowing on his cow-horn. He was still doing this in his early 80s, decades after Lois died.

Dan worked his own small farm and did a lot of the work on Uncle Ernest's much larger farm, for pay and/or a share of the crops. I'm not sure of the arrangement, but he rarely satisfied Uncle Ernest. He would go off fox-hunting or raccoon-hunting, or to drive Lois to the Holy Roller (Pentecostal) church up on the pike. Shouting and rolling her eyes back in her head and talking in tongues was Lois's chief delight in life. Dan was a gentle man who deferred to her wishes, not willing to let go and end up like his brother Clarentine, who was in the pen for killing a man. I didn't know any of Dan's siblings, but Mama said that Mrs. Collier had borne twenty-two children.

Dan and Lois had one severely afflicted son, Alvis, in a vegetative state, whom they always took in the car until later years, when Lois's nephew Woodrow would be charged with his caretaking. Alvis must have been in his teens, maybe older, when he finally died.

When Lois's brother Raymond Moubery (many comic English names in my neighborhood) lost his wife, the many motherless children were split up, Lois and Dan taking Woodrow, Myrtlene, and Thomas, then little more than a toddler. Woodrow was a good-natured, strong, big-footed country boy that Dan and Lois saddled with an unfair share of work. Myrtlene was a primitive, dark-tanned, pretty little thing, who would run around the corner of a building and squat down and pee in full view of anybody watching. (Myrtlene later married Alvin Breeden, of Earlysville, the only local resident I know who ever appeared on Garrison Keillor's *Prairie Home Companion.*) Lois spoiled her a bit. But it was Thomas that unplugged her dammed-up spoiling instincts. He was a rotten little kid. He called Myrtlene Butterbean and wanted her to ride him on the tricycle all of the time: "Ma, make Butterbean ride Sugarpie on the bicyc'." Uncle Ernest sneered and said, "More like Shitpie." He dubbed the boy Whistledick, or, sometimes softening it, Whistlepig.

Woodrow was clumsy and naive. Having no bicycle of his own, he sometimes rode ours, sometimes breaking something in the process. When he watched television with us at Uncle Ernest's, he talked to the cowboys: "Look out! He's right up there above you, behind that 'ere rock." We'd say, "He can't hear you, Woodrow."

When I was in my teens, Dan would drop Lois off at the house to visit with Mama while he drove to the general store to hang out with the others. Lois, who looked a bit like Popeye's Olive Oyl, wore near ankle-length dresses, usually of calico. She was all abuzz at this time because a nephew had married a girl from "JAY.pan," as Alberta's sons had married "EYE.talians." Natural xenophobia had teeth in it there in the countryside. One of the worst offenses anyone could be guilty of was being "from away from here." Bad enough to be from, say, Pennsylvania, but from JAY.pan?

Leaving the Colliers and the Mouberys, we return to the homeplace, a few hundred yards up the road from the outlet of Uncle Ernest's long, long driveway back over in the field. Directly opposite our house, across the dirt road, was the even longer drive, a half mile, perhaps, back to the Early place, facing toward what was called the Roach River on maps, what we called Ed Early's River, facing toward Albemarle County, close by.

Ed Early had died late in 1930, after the decennial census. Mama and Daddy had known him, and I knew him as a storied name but little about his actual life. Back in the nineteenth century he had married a woman from southside Virginia and fathered two children. His wife died around the beginning of the twentieth century, perhaps in childbirth. At any rate, she and her two children were buried in the family graveyard there on the Early place, a tangled, almost indecipherable tumble when I was a boy.

I didn't know until later that Fannie Davis was his second wife, married when she was around the age of 40, thus not single always like her siblings, Aunt Ruby's Bea and Boss. Decades after her husband died, she ran the place, inheriting, I think, well over 200 acres of good land and an almost-deaf, dotty sister-in-law, Miss Sarah Elizabeth Early, always known to us as Miss Sally-Betty. Fannie, with a cloud of white hair swirling around her head, and Miss Towne lived there at "Buffalo." (Ed Early's nickname was "Buffalo," why I don't know; somewhere I've seen a letter addressed to "Miss Towne, Buffalo" with the rest of the address.) The other two women seemed unduly harsh to Miss Sally-Betty, from an outsider's point of view. Miss Sally-Betty, biting on the corner of her straw fan, to help her hear, she said, was gentle and seemed to love children. Her hair was still mostly black when she was in her early 80s, and she outlived her sister-in-law quite a while, dying only a short time before Miss Towne, having moved with Miss Towne to a new house where the Marshalls used to live.

Having taught school locally for a while, at Celt, I think, Coolie Verner, now Dr. Coolie Verner, knew Fannie Early and came for long visits from time to time. If he came when school was in session, and Miss Towne happened to be a bit late to school, foul-mouthed fifth graders, fancying themselves full of worldly knowledge, would say, "I reckon Coolie Verner has her screwed to the bed." From this vantage point, I can say almost without a doubt that Dr. Verner was gay, often visiting with a young man in tow. Once when I was a teenager, such was my reputation of being a mechanical whiz (!—I could keep our newly acquired gasoline push mower running), Coolie asked me down to look at Miss Towne's push mower, talking incessantly about the magneto, while his young plaything stood to the side, helpless also, but smiling at me quite genially. I couldn't get the mower to run. In hindsight, however, I'd say there was a slight chance that Coolie's young man may have been revved up, so there's that at least.

(Quite recently, thanks to the Internet age, his picture showing him to be the man I knew [and how many Dr. Coolie Verners could there be anyway?], I discovered that Dr. Verner, born in China, thus the playful name, son of old Virginia tobacco farmers, was a world-renowned authority in adult education, rural sociology, and, especially, in the history of map-making. He became a cartobibliographer while working at the University of Virginia on some of Mr. Jefferson's maps and the early maps of Virginia. More surprising still, and I knew none of this in my youth, he had won a Purple Heart for disposing of bombs in Nazi-bombed London, later earning Queen Elizabeth's personal thanks for defusing a bomb in the crypt of St. Paul Cathedral. Greatness associated with Celt, and we generally snickered at the man, not knowing that he was a Fulbright Scholar, that he had studied art in Paris, that he was cartography's shining light in the 1950s, and that he would move his famous art collection to his self-designed home in the woods of British Columbia, where he taught at the university.)

Early on, Mrs. Early's tenant farmer, living in the field near a big rock about half the way down to the Early place, in a weathered, really small old house which looked rather like the Old House over on Uncle Ernest's place, was the often-drunk Herman Raines. He was a hard worker, genial when sober, a florid-faced big man, with a wife, Beatrice, and four or five children, though I can remember the names of just three—Shirley (Kay's buddy), the younger Geraldine, and my buddy for one school year, Awood (a Cockney form of "Haywood"?).

Kay was indebted to Beatrice for showing her how to make quick pickled beets, with cider vinegar and sugar. Awood showed me the place in the red road bank, a little cave-like hole under a partly-exposed tree root, where he went to hide when his father was drinking. The Raineses were not tenants for very long, perhaps his drinking the cause of their leaving.

Not long afterward, Eddie Riner, looking like B. O. Plenty in Chester Gould's "Dick Tracy" comic strip, took over the tenancy. He had an older son, Raymond, and a daughter, Marie, who was in the same classroom at William Monroe as Larry and I were, in the sixth grade. Marie had a fine imagination and often heard panthers and other creatures down on the bottomland of Fannie Early's farm. Riner's common-law wife, not the mother of his children, was Myrtie Bell Hodges, nearly as big as Alberta Shifflett, wearing the same sort of Old Dutch Lady sunbonnet. I'm sure that Myrtie was not to be trusted around men. She often walked the long way to our spring to get a couple buckets of water, saying that her spring, right near their house, was not very good, that it ran low and muddy. I think maybe she was on a venture for any man she could find. She would sit there in Mama's kitchen, her dark eyes in her doughy face darting right and left. Once I heard Daddy's crude dictum to an older brother: that a man should not have a woman whose ass was broader than her man's. Myrtie Bell (as we usually called her) had an ass broader than any man I had ever seen at that time.

Returning to the gravel road (604) that ran by our house, going up the road rather than down, we find that our closest neighbors in that direction lived about a quarter mile from us, up beyond the woods at the end of our property line. When I was very young, George and Graydon Lamb's aunt Fannie Lou and her husband Journey (sp?) Riddle lived in an old house that sat up on a stacked-rock foundation like ours. But the house was a good deal more ramshackle than ours, the kitchen jutting out over a downgrade, about four feet in the air, with stacked cinder blocks leading to the back door. The siding was an ugly brown asbestos, I suppose, sheeting in faux brick, what we called Rubberoid. June and Kay visited Fannie Lou fairly often and liked her a good deal. Kay was especially impressed by their cling peach tree, what she called a "plum peach," which really was the best around.

When I was still a small boy, the Riddles moved away. A three-person Negro family moved in—the widowered Oscar Steppe, his son Hunter, and Hunter's perhaps-wife Julia. They became a big part of the neigborhood. Hunter Steppe became our regular barber, replacing John Courtney, who lived over a mile and a half away and still used hand clippers, and Norris Wood, not used often, a notorious drunk about a mile away, up the New Road. Oscar helped around the neighborhood especially at hog-butchering time. And Julia worked for a number of neighbors, especially for Uncle Ernest and Aunt Ruby, doing their washing and ironing.

Mama sometimes got her to help out, paying a pittance, I'm sure. Julia ate meals after the family, always drinking just water, by choice. She nearly always wore blue jeans. She had a short torso and long legs. Uncle Ernest's nickname for her was "High Pockets." Nearly every day she could be seen pushing her gear in a red wheelbarrow, going from place to place, working. She laughed a lot, the end of her laugh tapering off to a whine in the back of her throat. She looked rather more like an Indian woman than a Negro, with glistening hair, light skin, and high cheekbones.

Every few weeks Larry and I (and, on a different schedule, Daddy) went to get our hair cut. The Steppes had a television set, sometimes tuned in to "Life Begins at 80" when we were there. I remember Georgiana Carhart especially, whom I didn't like, 80-plus or not. (A Broadway actress, she had one of the permanent positions on the panel, along with Gertrude Stein's cousin Fred.) I remember also being puzzled why anybody would watch Bishop Fulton J. Sheen, who was sometimes on as we got our hair cut. We rather dreaded approaching the house if the old man was outside alone. Oscar always grabbed little boys, at least Larry and me, at the crotch and felt our wee-wees before letting us into the house. We succeeded in pulling away very quickly. We never told anybody about the groping, probably afraid of what would happen to the old man, who was harmless enough, we judged. But it was humiliating.

After some years of the Steppes' living there, a scandal changed things. Apparently Oscar somehow discovered that Julia was having sex with some neighborhood men. She boasted that she had slept with every man in the neighborhood (nearly all white) except "Mr. Abe Dulaney." I have no doubt that she slept with some, but I doubt that she slept with all. Many of them were quite elderly. Anyway, Oscar beat her mercilessly for ruining the family's name, and she left. Mama said that she was glad that the temptation was gone from the neighborhood, but I am fairly sure that a couple of my older brothers had already yielded. As the neighborhood historian, I probably didn't miss much of what happened on my beat.

Some years later, Hunter and Oscar—I think the older man was still alive—moved to Ruckersville, Hunter still barbering in a better shop.

Beyond the Steppes' house, the then-sparsely populated country road had only a few houses within the next mile, before we came to the little country store run by George and Carrie Marshall.

Before the New Road ran off to the left, about a half mile from home, there was only one other house when I was a small boy. A miserable little shack on the right-hand side of a washboard curve housed for a short while Elmer Reese Conley, the oldest of the Conley children from down the road, and his wife and several babies. Apparently it had once been a more thriving home, for a huge black-heart sweet cherry tree stood to the left side of the shack.

Turning left onto what we called the New Road, we find more houses than on Rt. 604, but we didn't walk that road nearly as often as that leading to the Marshalls' store. That way ultimately led to Dyke, where my paternal great-grandfather Jeremiah McMullen Baugher had lived. We knew many of the kids on this road, who went to Celt Elementary School, but did not usually hang out with them outside of school. The first house encountered I remember to have been that of Geneva and Vernell Morris, Vernell being one of four people in our class once I was promoted to the third grade, Geneva being one grade ahead. But they moved further up the road, living diagonally across the road from Glenda Lawson, also one grade ahead.

Before we got that far up the road, the Woods, some Marshalls, and the Britten Morrises lived, the Marshalls, I think, later comers. Jack Marshall was close to my age and was a likeable freckled kid, Tom Sawyeresque. A fairly large family of Woods lived off the road to the right. The oldest two, Billy and Edward, were friends of my older brothers. Norris and Hattie, the parents, were friends of my parents, Hattie often walking the mile or so to our house to visit with Mama, with several of the younger ones in tow, all boys except Ruth Ann. I remember that Hattie often pulled her breast out to nurse the latest young'un, embarrassing Larry and me, sending us scurrying. Norris, a hard drinker, had apparently forced Hattie to give away one of the older children, I don't know why. Mama brought up the fact fairly often, saying she would never give away a child for a MAN.

The Britten Morrises lived further on, Edward being ahead of Larry and me and Wilmer further back in school at Celt. Other names from farther up the road are Evelyn and Tommy Shifflett, Mae Garth, the large family of Lutie and Allie Shifflett, and Marie and Charlotte Knight, at the end of the road where our bus went. I think that D. P. and Thomas Wayne Chapman also lived in the area, but I don't remember where their house was. Thomas Wayne was there at Celt when Larry and I were, probably one grade behind. D. P. (Davis Plunkett [one –t or two?]), who drove our school bus when I was a freshman or sophomore, I think, was of course known to the neighborhood kids as Displaced Person Chapman, a little post-World War II joke.

Mae Garth, ahead of Larry and me at Celt Elementary, I knew a bit more than some of the kids, for we often rode with Miss Towne up to Wyatt Garth's fine home, Wyatt being, oddly enough, the woman, not her husband, who was Frank, I'm fairly sure. She was a pal of Miss Towne and taught at Dyke Elementary. Willie Garth, I think that was her name, another male-named woman, ran a little store nearby, reputedly carrying on an affair with our rural mailman. Driven away from the store once, or so we heard, the mailman said, "I've just come to see my baby." Mama said that maybe he just meant Willie, not necessarily her baby.

Coming back to Route 604 and continuing a half mile or more up the road, we find only three habitations in the second half of our trip to the sto', where we walked at least every few days. On the left, way back in the field, lived an elderly Negro couple, Bob and Doshie (pronounced DOE. shee) Blakey. Perhaps they had a child or children, but none were there in my day. I remember going there once with Mama to look at doors. I have no idea why, but the Blakeys had about a dozen nice quality exterior doors for sale, stored in a shed. Their house was nicer than ours really, but I had no idea how they had earned a living earlier. He drove an old black car, probably a Chevrolet. Their driveway, winding through some woods and coming out next to Grant Jackson's blacksmith shop, was long and fairly often traveled. The rheumy-eyed, whiskey-swilling old blacksmith lived with the Blakeys, but I don't know whether he was kin. The Blakeys and Jackson, unlike the Steppes, were very black black folk, the Blakeys rather genteel, Jackson quite a bit less so. He still made horseshoes and hammered out metal repairs on his anvil.

In the condescendingly mild racist manner of the place and time, we were instructed to call elderly Negroes aunt and uncle, so it was "Uncle Grant" and "Aunt Doshie," though we never called old Mr. Steppe "Uncle Oscar."

Further up the road lived the Waltons, Delmer (with an –e-, I think, rather than the usual –a-) and Yettie. His first wife was an Elliot, dead long before my time, I suppose. Delmer was related to Aunt Dolly's husband, Armon Walton. Yettie had no children, but Delmer had two daughters by his first wife, Maude and Ruth. When I was a boy Maude still lived there with her two children, Betty Lou and Roger Lee. Betty Lou was famous in the neighborhood for getting her tongue or mouth stuck to a frozen pump handle, just as in the movie *A Christmas Story*. When I was a teenager, Maude married a man from Oregon (why there in Celt?), Leo Fenner, and moved into a house they built a bit beyond the store.

When Mama walked to the store, she liked to sit and have a talk out with Yettie Walton. Delmer scarcely did anything except sit on the screened porch, and he would fetch Yettie out to talk if she was inside. Yettie always called her husband, quite unironically, "Mr. Walton." Yettie was a good audience for stories, constantly exclaiming, "You don't say!" Mama bought damson plums from Yettie each summer to make Daddy's favorite preserves.

Just a bit short of the store, way back over in the field on the right, lived Yettie's brother Carl Shifflett, his wife Lizzie (Elizabeth), and their brood of young'uns. Carl and Lizzie were both tall, skinny, long-necked, and Lizzie with red hair to boot. She had a hot temper and was quick to wield a shotgun if she thought people were in her chinquapins or messing with her. Carl seemed to begin every third sentence with "The ole sayin' is" or "The ole sayin' was...." His nickname, consequently, was Ole Sa'in Is. He was unshakable, and Lizzie was likable if you didn't rile her. We liked hanging out there some. June would ride on the back of the truck with Carl's younger sisters, singing "Mama Don't 'Low No Guitar-Playing

Here" on the rare occasions when we attended an Evergreen Brethren Church revival. When a middle child of Carl and Lizzie, Ann, was asked in Bible school what her religious affiliation was, it was reported that she said, "Ma has seven toorkeys." It became one of our dozens of catch-phrases that delighted us.

George and Carrie Marshall and their son, Lewis, the hell-for-leather driver, ran the general store, just over a mile from our house. George seemed good-natured, rather slow-witted, with one hand missing. He worked in Charlottesville at a job which he wore a coat and tie for and drove a fairly late-model Chevrolet, his left stub resting on the steering wheel. He bought a new car every few years. Carrie was a sour-tempered misanthrope. (At the sto' the front-porch-sitting of the local men came later, during the tenure of Onnie Morris.) Carrie lavished what love she had, not on George but on her three jerkface little dogs, a Boston terrier and two chihuahuas, great American ankle-biters all, bullies only when one turned one's back on them.

George and Carrie had the first television set I knew of, and sometimes neighbors were allowed into the room behind the store to watch. I remember seeing Clayton Moore as the Lone Ranger and Hoagy Carmichael singing "Buttermilk Sky" as he accompanied himself on the piano. And I remember seeing there the coronation of Queen Elizabeth II.

We walked or, later, rode bicycles to the store for refreshments in good weather—a five-cent bottle of pop, always called just "a drink," a candy bar for the same price, or an ice cream bar, the same. Flush with work money, my older brothers would sometimes spend a quarter on a pint of Monticello Dairy ice cream, usually butter pecan. Sometimes we lugged a gallon of kerosene home, for fire-starting, especially in the kitchen stove. In an emergency, we would buy some sugar or flour or other staple there, but Mama much preferred to shop in Stanardsville, where she rode with Miss Towne.

When I was in my teens, Carrie—for reasons totally unknown to me—sent the sheriff to deliver a written notice to "Auger Baugher"—such was her semi-literacy—to stay away from her store. If she didn't want Olga Baugher, Mama, there, the sweetest person I knew, then I didn't much want to go there ever again.

Looked at from this distance, Carrie Marshall may be the subject of comedy. I wish I had known the word "misanthrope" at the time. I could have tossed the word at her as I exited the store with her hateful little dogs nipping my heels.

Beyond the general store, we knew a few people fairly closely, but it was not generally considered our neighborhood.

A little world of perhaps four square miles was the neighborhood of my youth. We found merriment there. We did not find high culture or the world of the intellect there, but we didn't want it, or—amounting to about the same thing—we didn't know that we wanted it.

Chapter 8

Specimen Days: Spring and Summer

When I was young, it seemed that each year there came a day or days in February that brought, in the fine words of Kenneth Grahame, "its spirit of divine discontent and longing . . ., calling imperiously," the same spirit that assailed Mole spring-cleaning underground. For Mole, it was really spring, and he could go roll in the meadows. For us, it was an illusion: February still had hidden tricks, no matter how gossamer its sleeves. I sat in the radiator-steam-heated classroom at William Monroe, almost certain that if I did not get out of geometry class (which I loved) and out under the luminous blue sky within the next fifteen minutes I would surely burst.

One pearlescent period in mid-February Daddy heard the same siren. He planted his potatoes, though that was usually done in our area on St. Patrick's Day. Mama warned him: "Now, Raleigh, you're getting ahead of yourself." A favorite saying tossed about in our household was "A hard head makes a soft ass," meaning that one is going to get a whupping, if only from fate and circumstance. Daddy went ahead and planted potatoes. February continued so warm that they came up. Then reality crept back, freezing all of the hardy little plants. A freeze while these Andean tubers are in the ground does little or no harm. But, shoot, there's a limit to above-ground hardiness. So Daddy had to replant. And I had to go back to the overheated classroom for more February days.

Then came March, finally stripping away the last of the leaves on the pin oaks. The farmer, had he been a Middle English poet, would have expressed his yearnings: "Western wind, when wilt thou blow,/ The small rain down can rain?" (In England, the western zephyrs bring spring rain.) Daddy yearned so: at least by the middle of March, earlier if possible, he got the ground plowed so that the small, thin, biting rain could penetrate the depths of the good loam. Early on it was Uncle Ernest with his team of horses, Maud and Nell, that plowed the ground of the fenced-in main garden; the large patch of ground beside the path to the barn, mostly for potatoes; the melon-growing patch just above the spring; the fenced-in patch behind the henhouse; and, nearly always, other smaller patches near the woodpile and between the house and Granddaddy's fruit orchard.

In the progression of the years, Dan Collier, with his horse-team, succeeded Uncle Ernest. Then Hoover, the most affable of the Conleys, broke the ground, ever so fast, with a plow and disc on his tractor. In later years, Daddy bought a Troy-bilt tiller to help with the cultivating work. For years and years, he used nothing much but a push plow, developing a rhythm lovely to behold: push the iron-wheeled cultivator right up to a corn hill, twist the wrist to dodge the plants, and onward, hour after hour, his mostly flannel shirts (even in mid-summer) soaked with sweat, his skin almost mahogany from the outdoor life, despite his brimmed hat. He was very vain of hearing young women driving by in cars stop to tell him he had the prettiest garden around.

The years scarcely slowed him, into his 70s, though by his late 70s he had Parkinson's Disease and might stumble without a plow to keep him from running away.

But it's early spring in the early '50s, Daddy's in his fifties and strong and hard-working, and I'm a young boy. (Daddy was 46 when I was born.) But not too young to be drafted to help with the tater-planting. After the earth had been plowed and, usually, disced and dried to a fine tilth, Daddy push-plowed the rows, as nearly parallel as if a mathematician scribed them. They were a perfect depth, with no impeding rocks to mention; the bags of potatoes were all cut, usually with a couple of eyes per piece; and the bags of fertilizer from Southern States sat unbroached. First, we spread fertilizer in the rows, so Daddy could come and push-plow the rows to mix the fertilizer and soil, with the straight plow-tip blade, not the turning blade or the cultivator/scratcher on. Then we set the potato starts.

Daddy at the age of 50; June, Larry, Roy with back to camera;
Hazel with her head in the trunk of their car.

Early on, Daddy still planted a few of the old, old standby, Irish Cobbler. Soon, they were supplanted by Kennebec, a great white potato still, and Red Pontiac or other ventures into the red-potato realm. That's it, but we would plant enough to yield at least 50 bushels probably. (Daddy sold some potatoes and gave some away to family.) We intended to set the potato pieces carefully, eyes up, about 14 inches apart, as he instructed. Tedious work, especially, makes young minds wander, and I would start thinking of Uncle Warren Harlow's story of a father calling out to his daughter, "Liza, get out of there. You know taters have eyes and you ain't got no drawers on!" My spacing of the seed potatoes would grow ever closer; Daddy would grouse a bit and space them correctly and then hand the bucket back. He was more tolerant in practice of a kid's fumbles than in theory and in what he would allow himself.

So far, spring has always come, sometimes by mid-March in Piedmont Virginia, sometimes closer to mid-April. The rejuvescence of the year, though probably not so spectacular as Minnesota's, is gaudy and noisy enough to satisfy most winter-jaded minds. Two of the first greens are willow trees' wispy ventures and daffodils, called "Easter flowers" where I grew up. Soon they are bobbing and nodding in the breezes. The surest sign that spring was "icumen in" was the incessant rackety chorus from down on the spring branch, near the pig pen, of spring peepers, little ole frogs singing away. This chirp that sounded like the stridulation of crickets led inevitably to anthropomorphic thoughts: they sounded as jubilant as any ring of elementary school chits.

We didn't sing reverdies, or write them either. But the re-greening continued apace. We planted onion sets, yard after yard of them marching single file—yellow, white, and sometimes red—lots of them to be eaten as spring onions, dipped in a small pile of salt on the edge of one's plate and bitten off, eaten with a forkful of buttery new potatoes, some grabbled out of the hills as soon as the plants bloomed. We planted "English" peas quite early, thickly twining around and around themselves, needing no pea brush for support. So they flopped over; so what? We children were indentured servants able to bend as low as necessary to pick them in early June.

A concave-edged triangle of land in the corner of the garden where the horse team could not plow was dug up with mattock or hoe and thickly sowed with Black-Seeded Simpson leaf lettuce, a lovely light green in almost no time. We didn't know we were being chic when, impatient, we ate baby lettuces, which would grow again if just pinched off. Mama had the same debate with herself every year: Did she like mayonnaise or sandwich spread best with lettuce? I knew that her absolute favorite was lettuce with spring onions, including the green tops, the onions cooked in bacon drippings just enough to shock them and then the grease poured over, to wilt the lettuce, the extra dressing to be mopped up with broken bread.

Puzzlingly, almost any time in March or April Easter came. We celebrated the primitive fertility rituals more than the Christian ones. Oh, we heard Tennessee Ernie Ford sing "Were You There When They Crucified My Lord?" ("Oh, sometimes it causes me to tremble, tremble, tremble") on the radio, but our real devotion was to Easter eggs, boiled whole Virginia hams, and coconut cake with home-canned peaches. Mama usually made lemonade, I think, for this holiday, the lemon slices swimming in the gallon crocks she used.

Larry and I at the Easter dinner table, 1958.

We were led in the secular direction by both school and home traditions. We usually dyed boiled eggs both places, favoring the Paas pastel colors fixed with vinegar. After a while, someone, both at school and at home, would start experimenting and get ugly browny-gray eggs, muddying the colors. Decals and wax pencil displacement of the colors fancied the eggs up, but we had no budding Faberge artists.

As my sister Kay observed, no matter how warm and splendid the days surrounding Easter were, the Sunday itself seemed to be raw and windy. We still spent hours hiding and re-hiding the eggs. Older brothers and sisters usually hid them for the younger members of the family, a self-sacrifice that was sometimes broken, but it was fun to hide them too.

Still, the real celebration of fecundity was growing things. By mid-April, usually, the air was redolent of lilac, the very fragrance of spring; the woods all around were white with dogwood and magenta with redbud; and by late April Daddy was rushing the season on things that might get nipped by frost until May 1. By then he had often planted dozens and dozens of little tomato seedlings. In the early years, he often got the seedlings from Uncle Ernest, who grew hundreds of them from saved seed, outdoors in old zinc wash tubs with the bottom taken out, the tubs filled with well-rotted manure and covered at night.

Since the seedlings were bare-root, they had to be coddled. We kids were bucket-bearers, pouring a big splash of water in each hole before Daddy shoved soil around the roots, moving on his overalled knees in the dirt from pre-dug hole to hole. After many, many dozen were planted, Larry and I had the hard job of cutting leafy branches from the trees on our place, the edge of Uncle Ernest's woods, down on the roadside, up on the school grounds, wherever, to shade the delicate plants for about a week. Most grew just fine, a few were replanted, all of them allowed to sprawl on the ground eventually, much of the time on oak-leaf mulch from Uncle Ernest's woods.

Daddy was generous, not to say sometimes prodigal, with the fertilizer, both manures and chemical. Chicken manure, especially, called for great care, so full of nitrogen that you could blast young growing things with too much of a good thing. Plants grew robustly under these ministrations, though Daddy tended to plant the same crops in the same places years in a row, starting with the lettuce in the roadside corner of the garden and moving inward from the road—onions and peas first, and so on, over to corn in the garden's middle, all of this for about two-thirds of the length of the garden, a hundred yards or so. Then, in blocks and shorter rows Daddy planted cucumbers, black-eyed peas, to be eaten green, green beans, limas, sweet peppers, squash, with lots of cabbage to eat green or for sauerkraut. The miscellaneity on the far side of the garden ran perpendicular to the center path.

The varieties planted make a study in horticultural history. The leaf lettuce was always Black-Seeded Simpson; the onion sets—always sets, never seeds—had no first name, just whatever was available in bulk in most country and town stores, labeled by color, though one could see what color the skins were. The "June peas" were often Wando or Laxton's Progress, perhaps even Lincoln. It didn't seem to matter much with peas. Edible-pod peas such as Sugar Snap were still in the future. Carrots we did not call by their first name. Daddy sowed them so thick, like almost everything, and never thinned them properly, so they mostly stayed small, spaced out some by the kids' pulling them to eat. A little earth eaten right with the orange pulp seemed to improve their flavor, and they needed no salt.

Beets were nearly always Detroit Dark Red or Crosby Egyptian, no being tempted by fancy beets with Italian or French names which, even today, I find not nearly so good as the old heirlooms. I've grown Chioggia, but no thanks: Crosby Egyptians are better for America. We always had lots more beets than carrots, always neighbors, root crops best planted in the early spring. Carrots not eaten fresh were diced and canned in pints, the only vegetable I remember being canned in pints only. These were destined for Mama's big pots of vegetable soup—tomatoes, lima beans, corn, onion, and carrots, almost always without any meat. Beets were canned in quarts or even in half gallons, eaten in winter straight out of the jar with salt sprinkled on or quick-pickled with vinegar, sugar, and a few spices. In the dizzy days of summer prodigality, we ate them mostly boiled and buttered.

The tomato seedlings were mostly well-known open-pollinated kinds whose seeds could be saved. Rutgers tomatoes were perhaps Daddy's favorite and remain one of mine. Big pink Ponderosa, some yellow tomatoes for Mama—too mild for most of us, who liked them acidy and sprightly—and some Marglobe, Oxheart, and Beefsteak were the main ones, no doubt with an experimental variety or two, including some pear-shaped little ones.

The beans were either bush or pole varieties. Green beans, then called, quite accurately, "string beans," were, nearly always, White Half-Runner, a light green bean still much prized in the Southern garden. When we picked several bushels at once for canning, we children fussed and fumed at all of the strings and beetle spots to be cut out. Pole beans, with all of their architectural fussiness of sticks and strings, were most likely Kentucky Wonder. Mama liked them mature, with what she called "goodies" in them, what deep Southerners sometimes call "shelly" beans.

Fresh lima beans—nearly as good as sweet corn, which, as any Garrison Keillor fan knows, stands right next to sex on the list of supernal human blessings—fresh lima beans, I say, had to be Henderson Bush Baby Limas to be the very best. Still, speckled lima beans, in all patterns of red and purple and greeny-white, were fun to shell, barring a bit of painful shell fiber's getting shoved up too far under one's fingernails. However, they turned an unfortunate browny-gray when cooked, but still tasted good.

Early on, Daddy still grew some white corn, the very long-season Stowell's Evergreen being the usual. Then he switched to mostly yellow corn, Golden Cross Bantam being the main crop. Neither the stalks, seven feet tall, nor the ears, full size for my hands, ever seemed to be bantam, but we ate without fretting. The farm cats came running when they heard the first ear being shucked, and we tossed them the faulty ends of the ears and an occasional full ear. We had one family of cats that loved raw cantaloupe along with the raw corn. They would eat it right down to the rind if we cut the pieces small enough. I have thrust many a slice of cantaloupe at cats since, but they apparently lack the necessary gene: they wince and draw back, as if to say, "Cats don't like fruit!" In later years Daddy would plant some bi-color corn and of course the later-developed Silver Queen. From July on, we had corn nearly every day. Nobody ever complained. Daddy was weird: he often ate corn-on-the-cob with only a bit of salt sprinkled on. The rest of us knew that corn had to be dripping with butter, with plenty of salt AND black pepper sprinkled on. Cut-off-the-cob corn also graced the table often, alone and simmered in milk or combined with limas and, sometimes, tomatoes.

Squash were of two kinds: yellow crookneck or pattypan, which Mama always called cymlings. The kids didn't relish squash much—and thankfully we were spared zucchini—but Mama did. No okra, despite our Southern bona fides, no eggplant, no winter squash beyond pumpkin.

When the soil was wholly warmed up, Daddy planted sweet potatoes and melons. The sweet potatoes (never so-called "yams," which don't grow in Virginia [Never mind a cannery getting the guvmint to allow the label for the orange sweets.]) were often gotten as starts from Dan Collier, or store-bought, most of them Puerto Ricans. We rarely got to see sweet potato blooms, by which we could see how closely kin to morning glories they are, for Daddy would always get us to cut back the exuberant growth to feed to the cows for a late-summer treat. I tried later to get him to stop this olden practice, but science and facts about photosynthesis and the storage of food in the below-ground tubers did not move him. He scoffed at my ideas. The closest I came to convincing him was by analogy: "Would you cut off the tops of your potato plants?" Still, stubborn, he was satisfied with lots of really small sweet potatoes, robbed of their top-growth for weeks on end.

The watermelons, always planted in hills, in a cross-shaped furrow drawn with Daddy's forefinger, were sometimes giants: Congo, Tom Watson, Black Diamond, Dixie Queen. In later years, he would often plant the distinctly inferior Sugar Baby. We didn't need "icebox" melons; we needed them as big as we could get.

Cantaloupes were of several kinds, orange and green. We never planted honeydews, but Rocky Ford, a smaller, green-fleshed (tinged with orange next to the seed cavity) cantaloupe was the universal favorite. One of my brothers-in-law could never be persuaded to try the green-fleshed melon. His loss. It's still the best cantaloupe I've ever et.

In late summer, after the potatoes were dug, Daddy planted turnips in the space, purple-topped ones only. We ate them raw mostly, heavily salted. Mama simmered them in milk, and we sometimes had turnip greens. Cows got the huge surplus, coming to full growth when grass was winding down.

When spring was in full swing, especially after May 1, when we shucked our shoes for the home-season, we spent lots of our free time in inherited or self-invented family games outdoors. We still played card games and a few board games indoors at night, but those were mostly cool- and cold-season diversions. With a family of nine children, there were usually enough people for pick-up games of all kinds.

A few games were mostly gender-specific, but the lines were never strictly dawn, especially by the time we got to the end of the line of kids: Kay, Larry, and I would play anything together. Kay and June excelled at "girl" games that required dexterity with the fingers, such as pick-up sticks and jack-rocks. Still, others would try, until the boys grew tired of getting beat. These games were often played on the kitchen/dining room table, even in good weather, but when the weather was fine, we got right down in the beaten dirt, sweeping away any roughness that would make the little ball bounce awry. (Like many poor Southern homes, we had places around the house where grass never grew, the ground being so hard trod by many feet. Later, grass covered it all.) We later boys also essayed hopscotch, played with a flat piece of broken glass, the only special equipment required, other than a stick to draw the boxes in the dirt. Again, Kay mostly won, but upsets were cause for elation.

We were attracted to marbles, played in my father's boyhood as a very serious game. He still had a small collection of large clay marbles that we were sometimes allowed to play with, but they scarcely rolled true. Mostly the boys in the family played marbles, but again, there were really no gender lines. We did not use the elaborate big circle rings of formal marbles in earlier times but scribed a square in the dirt with a marble at each corner and one marble in the center of the square where intersecting diagonals crossed. The biggest sin in marbles was to "hunch" or "hoke" the shooting marble, not letting it go soon enough, guiding it too far toward the marble we aimed at. Larry, it seemed to me, was always hoking the marble, and he said that I always hoked it.

Scarcely ever did girls in the family join in on mumbly-peg, an old, old game of tossing a pocket knife in the air. Roy and Carl mostly played this, allowing Larry and me to join in, under close supervision, down behind the meathouse. One opened a blade at either end of the knife and then a third blade, a small one, at right angles to the other two. A spinning toss of the three-bladed knife won points according to how the knife's blades stuck into the sod or soil on landing. No one was ever cut or maimed, as I recall, but I understand why we played behind the meathouse, away from Mama's eyes.

The clotheslines were strung behind the meathouse, the clothes wind- and sun-kissed all times of the year. In fine weather Mama would allow us to use a sheet or blanket from the wash as a makeshift pup tent. We lowered the wooden line props enough to let the sheet drag in the grass. Especially in the long shadows of late afternoon, or "evening," as all hours after noon until dark were called where I grew up, such tents were fun to bide in to play sedentary guessing games or to read books in when the summer grew long. Sometimes we read magazines there, most often hand-me-down *Saturday Evening Post, Life, Look, Collier's,* or *Coronet* from Daddy's first cousin once-removed Jollett Steppe or from Uncle Ernest's children. In slower times, when it was warm we made our way gradually through the stacks of old magazines in Uncle Ernest's back-back-room, under the sloping roof, up the staircase with no balusters or banister. Most of these dated from World War II, where I absorbed most of my knowledge of that big conflict, our history classes in school rarely getting that far.

When we had enough people, when young relatives visited, or neighbors like Jimmy and Kenny Marshall, we could mount a town ball game in the cow pasture across the fence from the clotheslines or, better yet, up on top of the hill above our spring, the highest spot on our land, tolerably flat, and with a panoramic view of the Blue Ridge Mountains as backdrop to our game.

A family game that I've never heard of elsewhere was Annie Over. A team, as small as two to a side, as large as we could gather, would stand on either side of the older part of our house, the stem of the T. With a soft ball—a hollow rubber ball or a tennis ball—in hand, a player would yell "Annie," a player on the other side would yell "over," and then the one with the ball would throw it over the house. There would be a lull as the other side caught or chased down the ball. One player held the ball behind his back, disguising who had it, all players on the team running around both ends of the house while the team that threw the ball tried to figure out who had the ball, running around the house in the opposite direction, trying to avoid being hit by the ball thrown by the opponent. I think that anyone hit by a ball then had to go to the other team. The game ended when all players on one side had been hit. A really high-tech game. It served its main purposes: getting to yell, throwing a ball, feinting, and hitting someone with a ball. (My colleague Dennis Gartner tells me that he played a game like this, called "Eenie, Einie Over," I think, growing up in North Dakota about the same time.)

When I was in high school, when only Larry and I of the nine kids were left at home, I made a game that was tons of fun. I was often trying to make things, sometimes without the necessary tools, materials, and expertise. But box hockey was a game that I made that gave us a fast and furious workout. Of all the sport-like games we ever played, it was the lone one in which I had a slight winning edge over Larry.

When in high school, we sometimes pitched horseshoes at home. However, that game was spoiled by Dan Collier, drawn ineluctably to the game and able to beat any kid in the countryside. Let him just hear the unmistakable clank of metal on metal and he was there, though a quarter mile away when we started pitching.

We had bicycles, nearly always up and running. When Kay, Larry, and I were left as the only at-homes, we discovered that we could clear away the years and years of accumulated leaves in the woods of Uncle Ernest's place near our garden, in the small section of land between his draw-bars and the road. We pushed the leaves and leaf-mold to the side of a dizzying network of roads we made and rode our bicycles hour after hour. The wood was full of big trees, mostly oak, and many saplings, which had the trick of magnetically drawing one's bicycle toward them and scraping one's elbows or making the bicyclist come a purler, bouncing off the sapling, sometimes going ass over teacup onto the ground. But what is childhood without scrapes and scabs?

We made little rooms off to the side of the bike trails, perhaps with a bench of scrounged wood laid in tree forks. Kay was always flush, buying crackers, potted meat, and Kool-Aid for us to feast on, with lots of penny candy such as B-B Bats, Mary Janes, and Squirrel Nut Zippers to polish off the snack, and then back on our bikes.

Next to being in motion, most kids like making noise. We would take a break from cycling in the woods to make an impromptu kazoo. Lots of mountain laurel grew in these woods (locally known as "ivy," disturbingly). A short piece of laurel wood, the size of a small kid's finger, was carefully split in two and then, for reed, we inserted a laurel leaf and trimmed it to fit the diameter of the twig and length of the split. Holding the instrument like a flute and blowing on it with the proper embouchure, we had our music noise.

Uncle Ernest seemed to look askance at our trails and rooms, but a good sport nearly always, he said nothing except in his facial expressions. So we took that as license to continue until we tired of the diversion. Of course, we had said nothing about the road engineering until we had already done it.

Spring and high summer drew lots of visitors, many of them coming in cars and trucks to visit the mostly no-four-wheels Baughers. Since we lived on the old Baugher homeplace, where Daddy and his six siblings grew up, and since Mama's parents and four of her five siblings lived nearby, the most numerous visitors were family. Sometimes the visitors were rather remoter family.

One of my favorite anecdotes involving visitors happened one summer when I was small. Two young women, Daddy's distant cousins I think, were talking, quietly they thought, about Mama. Never the best of housekeepers but with her main priorities straight, Mama often let the house go when she could not keep up. She often couldn't keep up in the summer because of the task of feeding a constant stream of visitors. One of the women said, quite unfairly and no doubt untruthfully, "This is the filthiest house I've ever been in." Daddy's hearing, later very bad, was keen enough to hear them talking in the hall next to the bedroom. He snapped back at them, "Not half so filthy as since you two whores walked in." Daddy would not have talked that way to Mama's relatives, but he had no hesitation in talking to HIS relatives that way, if the offense was sufficient. You may be sure they didn't hang around long.

What I most remarked, half-knowingly then and with full glee now, was the oddity of lots of names of the people that visited or that Mama and Daddy knew in the area. Delward Weaver Shifflett was one of our next neighbors down the road. The next neighbor up the road when I was a very small boy was Journey Riddle. One of Daddy's oldest friends, and old workmate, was Raymond Clatterbuck, almost as good a name as Benedict Cumberbatch, had Raymond's first name been better. A neighbor through the fields beyond Uncle Ernest's farm was Whitelaw Snow. Further names for the collector were Bez Snow, Tobe Gentry, Moze or Mose Lawson, Cleveland Raines, and Bluey Shifflett. These are given on the census forms as the real names, not nicknames.

Some of Mama's friends and acquaintances were Minnie Roudabush, as Mama still called her, relishing the name apparently, though she had been Minnie Powell for decades by that time; Nelie (pronounced NEE. ly) Wampler; Wyatt and Willie Garth, both women; Loney Conley and Ressie Roach, her daughter; Ackline Deane, a county official with dignity to match her name, and from Mama's youth, in the neighborhood where she grew up, which Daddy always called Scuffletown, over on the road to Quinque, an old Colored woman named Molly Mozee (perhaps spelled Mauzy, like the Shenandoah Valley town across the mountains). When Mama stretched and yawned, she often said, "Oh my, oh me, Molly Molly Mozee." I didn't know she was a real woman until I was a bit older. I've earlier mentioned the Extension Agents of the 4-H clubs, Miss Violet Navy (the "Miss" always there) and Bogardus Worth.

The favorite talk of many visitors, apparently just a-hankering to do some amateur doctoring or else suffering from lots of hidden ailments, was of patent medicines like Hadacol, with its high percentage of alcohol, and, even more often, of home-bred quackery. Mama limited her medical talk mainly to comparing the relative merits of Yeager's Liniment and Porter's Liniment. Liniments, of course, have real value for aching muscles. Mama must have had more aches than we kids thought about. But most of the best talk was pure quackery. One man, I've forgot who or what the ailment treated was, recommended buying empty capsules and painstakingly filling them with Dreft washing powder. I assume the aim was some sort of cleansing or detox (that hokum around even then). The man specified, "Now it has to be Dreft," the new detergent used for washing clothes or dishes. Liquid dishwashing soap must have been around then, but we seemed to use the same product for clothes and dishes, sometimes powdered detergent, sometimes home-made lye soap, sometimes Octagon bars.

Another visiting quack, treating some stomach ailment, recommended scraping all of the white pit from oranges and ingesting that, perhaps in capsules, but I don't remember just how. More likely to cause a stomach complaint than cure one, I thought. But my sister June always told me that my trouble was that I was a skeptic. Later, I would answer proudly, "Damn straight."

For a while, beginning when I was perhaps 6 or 7, we had a traveling sawmill on our place and was thus visited fairly often by Mr. (the only first name I remember) Glass and his "afflicted" grown son, John. Mr. Glass ran the sawmill over in our woods, down a rubble-rock road beyond the drawbars up the road near the western end of our property. Down this road Uncle Ernest would drive his wagon and team to fetch home for us lengths of polewood to be sawed for "stovewood," pronounced "sto'wood," the smaller firewood used in the kitchen stove.

A few hundred yards down this road, near the edge of the woods, adjacent to the cow pasture, the big-deal sawmill was set up. It made a mountain of sawdust, still there when I was in my mid-twenties, so must have been there for a good while. What the lumber sawn was used for I do not remember. Could this have been the lumber that Uncle Jinks used to build our fine new barn? It seems to be later than that. Or did Daddy sell the lumber to earn some ready money from the fine oak and pine and poplar that grew in our woods? Mr. Glass was the only itinerant sawmill operator I ever knew.

He either had lots of business conversations with Daddy or just liked visiting, for he was at the house fairly often, a genteel-acting white-haired man with rimless eyeglasses. But his son John always came with him, Mrs.

Glass rarely or never. We children would peep around the corner into Mama and Daddy's bed/sitting room, where John sat on the daybed while Daddy and Mr. Glass talked. Seeing us, he would grin, an expression that we found full of malignant intent when he drew his finger across his throat, signifying that he was going to slit our throats if he got the chance. Mama and Daddy didn't seem to pay any heed to his threats, so we would run and try to take care of our own lives. Mildred and Patricia were visiting at least once when the Glasses were there. They were just as terrified as we were, so it was sound kid sense to be so.

From April on, through the lazy, fly-buzzing days of high summer, Daddy would pay little heed to visitors he didn't like if they didn't want to listen to the baseball Game of the Day that he had on the radio each afternoon. He usually got up shortly after dawn (4 a.m. standard time at midsummer) and worked in the garden before breakfast and again after, gathering produce or cultivating the crops as the heavy dews dried. By dinner time of day, mid-day, he had done most of a day's work. After eating, he lay down to read the newspaper, any magazine, or pulp fiction he had on hand, and dozed off and on with the baseball game as constant background to lazy afternoons. There weren't so many night baseball games then, with only eight teams in each of the two major leagues. The Cubs' Wrigley Field had no night-lights, so all of their home games were day games. The hapless Senators were in Washington; the Browns in St. Louis; the Braves in Boston; the Giants in New York; the Dodgers in Brooklyn. The Pittsburgh Pirates were eternally in the cellar, but they had Ralph Kiner; the Senators had Harmon Killebrew, and the Braves Warren Spahn.

Dizzy Dean, pitching ace of the St. Louis Cardinals in the '30s, semi-literate but an entertaining radio announcer, would break into a lull in the game to sing a verse or two of "The Wabash Cannonball," and Daddy would start half-awake and ask Larry what had happened while he was asleep. Larry could give him a blow-by-blow report, even if we were outside playing with kittens wrestling each other or making roads in the dirt to run our wood-block makeshift cars through. To me it was more like background noise, featuring the boys of summer (both the baseball players, as Roger Kahn dubbed them, and us, doing our thing).

But I knew lots of players. Larry and I collected baseball cards, and most of the family picked teams to root for: Daddy and Larry for the New York Giants (Daddy later for the new Baltimore Orioles), Carl for the Cleveland Indians, Roy for the Brooklyn Dodgers, Kay for the Chicago White Sox, and I rooted for the Boston Braves. We almost forgave Uncle Ernest his rooting for the New York Yankees. The Yankees! Had he no soul? The biggest hit on Broadway relevant to baseball was *Damn Yankees!* with the splendid Gwen Verdon, and the title sentiment resonated.

Uncle Ernest and Uncle Sidney shared Daddy's baseball mania. In the '50s the Braves moved from Boston to Milwaukee. When big Joe Adcock hit four homeruns in one game, the prowess delighted Uncle Ernest as if the Braves had been his team. Joe Adcock may still have some power records standing since the 1950s. This smashing hitter gave Uncle Ernest an excuse for some off-color jokery: thereafter, Uncle Ernest never referred to him except as "Big Cock," even in The Year That the Yankees Lost the World Series to the Braves (1957).

Baseball cards came in packs of tough ole sheet bubblegum, and too often, instead of Eddie Mathews or Roy Campanella, Larry and I got yet another copy of Felix Mantilla, Wayne Terwilliger, or Zoilo Versalles. Still, we collected quite a few cards, filling most of the space in two shoe boxes. We had early Willie Mays, Mickey Mantle, Eddie Mathews, and Gus Triandos, of the new Baltimore Orioles, founded on the ruins of the defunct St. Louis Browns team. The collection, left at home when we grew up, must have been worth a fair amount, but when I searched for the cards years later I found that apparently the children living there seem to have destroyed them all.

Soon we had other reasons to listen to the radio, especially in summer, when we could plug the old AM or the newfangled FM radio into our only outdoor electrical outlet, just outside the kitchen door. My brother-in-law Joe Clayson installed it. We had had battery radios even before the house was electrified. So the Carter Family, Uncle Dave Macon, Hank Williams, and Grandpa Jones were well-known even before we had "our" (Larry's and my) music. In the mid-fifties rock and roll rose like thunder out of the bay of pop music and blues. Our family had mostly listened to country, or hillbilly, music. Since the mid-40s Fred, especially, had liked the new "bluegrass" music of Bill Monroe and his followers. I remember saying in the early fities that my favorite singer was the country, country, country Webb Pierce. But not for long.

June had always liked a number of pop singers, especially the exquisite Jo Stafford. We weren't especially shaken by Bill Haley, but then in 1956, just as Larry and I were about to enter high school, there were Gene Vincent, Elvis Presley, Pat Boone (before he lost his voice and became a right-wing, evangelical twit), Fats Domino, Chuck Berry, the Everly Brothers, and soon Jerry Lee Lewis, Eddie Cochran, Roy Hamilton, Bo Diddley, and Buddy Holly. Alongside these were the more traditional pop singers like Perry Como, Patti Page, Tony Bennett (sometimes doing Hank Williams), and the Ames Brothers, all of whom we liked too. Daddy, grumbling and grousing about our radio choices, as always, singled out Perry Como of the whole lot to cuss about. Perry Como! We wondered, Has he never heard Bo Diddley? Larry Williams ("Bony Moronie" for one; "Short Fat Fannie")? Little Richard?

I had always disliked the Big Band sound just prior to my pop music consciousness, and especially Frank Sinatra. Tony Bennett I tolerated just fine, and who could dislike the singing of Doris Day? Still, Fats Domino's "Blueberry Hill" and Chuck Berry's "Sweet Little Sixteen," perhaps the most vibrant and bouncy new song I had ever heard, roused me to a whole new world. The Weavers and Miriam Makeba were around then, but I wouldn't discover true folk music until I went to college. Now it was "Hail, hail, rock and roll!" And lots of other kinds of music coexisting on the pop stations.

Not that we ever went to dances or anything. I was only 12 years old, after all, even if we weren't too shy, or had a way. But we could spend half-hours dipping our combs in glasses of water and getting the D. A. at the back just so. Larry, with somewhat curly hair still, trained a spit curl down right over his right eye. We jigged around mostly outdoors, away from Daddy's sight, the radio on high outdoor volume.

The fifties were a good decade to come to full musical consciousness. We heard, on the same radio station, many different kinds of music: Les Paul and Mary Ford, Earl Grant, Mitch Miller's Colonel Bogey March from *Bridge Over the River Kwai,* Roy Hamilton's "You Can Have Her"; new versions of old standards like "Unchained Melody," "Ebb Tide," and the smooth wonder of The Platters in "Smoke Gets in Your Eyes"; country and country-tinged material like Jo Stafford doing Hank Williams, Johnny Horton, Jim Lowe, Jim Reeves, Chet Atkins, Sonny James, Marty Robbins, Tennessee Ernie Ford, Jimmy Dean, Ferlin Husky, Don Gibson, Johnny Cash, and Guy Mitchell. We heard Conway Twitty before he went country; we heard exotica like Martin Denny's "Quiet Village"; we heard Brook Benton, the best singer to listen to in a car on back-country roads; we liked most of the almost-operatic Jackie Wilson.

How is this for a random list of eclectic big hit-makers from the late 1950s? Clyde McPhatter, Sarah Vaughan, Little Richard, Jane Morgan, Frankie Laine, Sheb Wooley, Sam Cooke, Johnnie Ray, Della Reese, the Big Bopper, Connie Francis, Ray Charles, Dean Martin, Kay Starr, Harry Belafonte, Neal Sedaka, Peggy Lee, Andy Williams, Nat King Cole, Georgia Gibbs, Dinah Washington, the McGuire Sisters, Eddy Arnold, Domenico Modugno, Johnny Mathis, Gogi Grant, and Bing Crosby and Grace Kelly, for heaven's sake. And we cannot forget the marvel that straddled country and really high-tone orchestral music, Ray Price.

I'm talking eclectic, especially when such a variety of instrumentals was the rage. In the early fifties we had had the country-tinged, ragtime-tinged piano of the fabulous Del Wood ("Down Yonder"). By the mid- and late fifties, add the jazzy Bill Doggett ("Honky Tonk"), the twangy guitar of Duane Eddy ("Rebel Rouser"), the forever-active Nelson Riddle ("Lisbon Antigua"), Bill Justis ("Raunchy"), Hugo Winterhalter ("Canadian Sunset," with Eddie Heywood on piano), Morris Stoloff ("Moonglow") segueing into the theme from "Picnic"), even electric organ hits (Dave "Baby" Cortez). Les Baxter, Jimmy Dorsey, Leroy Anderson, Billy Vaughn (many hits for Dot records), Ray Anthony, Roger Williams, the Champs, Percy Faith, Santo and Johnny, Reg Owen, Sandy Nelson, Cozy Cole, and Perez Prado had hits, wrestling for place with the likes of the Coasters, the Rays, Laurie London, and the Dell-Vikings.

In the daytime we favored Harrisonburg's WHBG on AM, just across the Blue Ridge Mountains, but it signed off at sundown, a sepulchral voice intoning every day, I kid you not, the opening quatrain of Thomas Gray's "Elegy Written in a Country Churchyard." There they were, "Tutti Frutti" cheek-by-jowl with "The curfew tolls the knell of parting day." Twentieth-century raunch and eighteenth-century poetry. At night, when the airwaves were overtaken by the bigger and GREAT BIG stations, we listened mostly to WINC and WRFL AM/FM, from Winchester, Virginia, and to WKBW, Dick Biondi, from Buffalo, New York, an early wild-man DJ (apparently still DJing in his eighties as I write, now in Chicago!) I don't remember the name of the main DJ we listened to on the Winchester station. I do remember that he said that he was coming to us with our flat friends, platters and transcriptions.

Sometimes we watched the early days of Dick Clark's "American Bandstand" on TV at Uncle Ernest's. But it was always a faintly embarrassing show to us, full of Philadelphia silliness, emphasizing the crappiest of rock performers—Danny and the Juniors, Paul Anka, Bobby Vee, Bobby Rydell, Frankie Avalon.

Lying on my belly at the window of the bedroom Larry and I shared, a double iron bedstead for each of us, the cool summer night breezes wafting into the dark room, with only the glow of the radio dial, with everything from Patsy Cline to Frogman Henry, from Gale Storm to Stan Freberg, from the Kingston Trio to the Chordettes, from the Impalas— "Sorry (I Ran All the Way Home)"—to Lloyd Price, Dinah Washington, Billy Grammer, Bobby Darin, the Diamonds, and Rick Nelson keeping us company, I felt sure that I could levitate and just float there in the air.

Mama was always so grounded in hard work, cheerfully singing hymns, that she was in no danger of floating away. She didn't mind what we listened to on the radio as we worked. Late spring and all summer long, hard work, coming in spurts, was there to do. The most demanding of tree fruit, tart cherries, the first to mature, around the end of May or first of June, was everybody's favorite. We always had at least a dozen trees, along the garden fence near the house, around the meathouse, and near the woodpile. I think that they were Early Richmond cherries, seedlings from Granddaddy Baugher's original fruit, springing up all around, allowed to grow to fruition if not in the way too much.

For me as a boy picking sour cherries meant climbing up into the trees with a gallon plastic bucket. Woe to the picker who had a scratch or some little wound on the hands or arms: the acid juice would run down one's arm as he reached for cherries above his head. The juice was sticky also, evincing that there was sugar in the fruit, though hard to discern when eating them raw. We seeded all of the cherries by hand, watching for bad ones as we squeezed. Soon we learned that the seeded fruit, after sitting a while in a gallon crock, seemed sweeter than the cherry sucked right off the stem. Mama, mostly a rather slow worker, worked far faster than we kids did in seeding the fruit. She always made at least one cherry pie each time we were seeding for canning. The trees bore wonderfully well just about every year, with no special care, and we canned many dozen half-gallon jars of cherries, the first fruit of the year to go into the closet under the stairs. We had no freezer then, so all of the cherries that weren't used fresh were canned or turned into preserves, which never lasted long, cherry being my absolute favorite. Pies from canned cherries aren't quite so good as those from fresh or frozen cherries, but to my mind sour cherry pie is still the best pie that exists. Instead of a birthday cake, I was later to ask for a cherry pie, October or not. In winter, we ate the canned cherries in bowls with as much added sugar as we dared.

Once, Larry and I, hungry for cherry pie before they were fully ripe, made a little one while Mama was in Stanardsville getting groceries. The crust and the whole pie were quite imperfect, since I made the dough from memory of watching Mama. Mama said, and appeared to be quite sincere, that it was the best cherry pie she had ever eaten, that the cherries being under-ripe just added to the taste. I'm sure that we added enough sugar to compensate for the under-ripeness.

From July, when Early Transparent apples ripened, until November, when Staymans and Granddaddy Baugher's Black Twig apples were ready, we canned apple sauce. Mama's apple pies were actually applesauce pies, no matter when made. When we made apple butter, we got apples from elsewhere, sometimes the drop apples from the huge orchards of the Byrd family, Virginia politicians and writers from colonial days and huge apple orchardists.

The other fruit canned in great quantities, peaches in August, were bought from orchards, mostly in Crozet or Orange. We had a few peach trees, but the fruit was mostly uncertain, small, knotty, but good to eat fresh. Of wild fruit, we canned many half-gallons of blackberries, mostly eaten by the bowlful, since fresh ones made much better pies.

When the kitchen was to the left of the hall, at the front of the house, it was always hot, for canning in a water bath canner that held only seven half-gallon jars at a time took countless hours of keeping the wood stove stoked. The floor near the door nearly always had at least a dozen jars sitting on sheets of newspaper cooling so that the rings could be removed and re-used. Then the jars went into the closet, hundreds of them—half gallons, quarts, and pints.

Of the vegetables canned in high summer, corn and lima beans were the most problematic. Not often but sometimes a jar of tomatoes would spoil, but only corn and lima beans would have a bad jar out of every twenty or thirty canned, whether because of low acidity or a few bad beans or grains of corn or what, it was still a betrayal of one's hard work. I don't remember green beans, beets, carrots, applesauce, or cherries ever spoiling. We also canned quite a bit of tomato juice, fixing a batch every few days at summer's end, but its acidity protected it; it was the quickest way with tomatoes; and it didn't even need a hot-water bath for hours.

In addition to canning enough produce to last us through a long winter and cooking three meals a day, doing the wash and some ironing, cleaning and so on, Mama, especially in the early years of my life, made some of the clothes that we wore and milked the cows twice a day.

I don't know when we got our treadle Singer sewing machine—perhaps in the early '40s when Daddy was working in the shipyard during the War. It appears in my memory to have been a new one, not used, though it saw hard use for years. Mama made some dresses, skirts, and blouses that the girls wore, and some for herself. Most of the patterns were probably from Simplicity, McCall's, and Butterick, often spread out for the cutting here and there around the house. She made a few shirts for Larry and me, and cut off pants to make shorts, which we lived in during the summer. This was the age of printed feed sacks. One would select just what bag of chicken laying mash she wanted by the pattern on the bag, wash it well when all the mash had been fed, and then make some article of clothing. Mama mostly made aprons from this mainly flowery material. Most of her aprons, which she did not always wear, were over-the-neck full ones, using rick-rack or other ornamental tapes on key edges.

Needing no electricity, the sewing machine sat in the downstairs hall, where there was no outlet. So most sewing was done in the summertime, for there was also no heat there in the hall. As Daddy's rhythm with the push plow was a pleasure to watch, so Mama's rhythm with the sewing machine was: turn the wheel to get the needle moving a bit and then pedal the treadle steadily, guiding the material just as one would with an electric sewing machine, but requiring a more definite rhythm and getting a leg-muscle workout.

Mama was interested in reading and hearing about all sorts of needlework, but other than hand-sewing, a little bit of tatting, and a tiny bit of crocheting, she didn't do it. She never knitted. Leisure time—what's that? She did almost no darning but would hand-sew little rips.

Mama did not milk at the crack of dawn. She milked after cooking and eating breakfast. The cows could wait. In summer, in the afternoon the cows would sometimes retreat to the woods and little streams. She would call the cows, "Soooooookeee, soookee," and the cows would usually come. If not, kids went to drive them home. In the finest of weather, when the cows did not need a scoop of dairy feed to bribe them, Mama would take her three-legged stool and milk the cows as they munched grass in the pasture, though she had to move occasionally or smack the flat of the hand on the cow's haunch, saying, "Saah, Cherry"; "Bossy! Bossy! Saaahhh!"

When some kids reached a certain age, they helped with the milking. Still, it has to be admitted, Mama did most of it, even when she had help.

Gail, my sister Violet's oldest child, only 7 1/2 years younger than I was, the first grandchild, spent lots of time at the homeplace in summer, from the time she was about three. She loved going to the barn or out into the pasture with Mama while she milked *al fresco*. Once Uncle Ernest's bull was over in our pasture and was having erotic thoughts while the cows were being milked. Mama was not the least bit afraid of the bull, even when the cows were "bullin'," as we called it. Gail looked at the bull and asked, "Grandma, why does that cow have a carrot sticking out of its belly?" Not one to lose her *sangfroid* just because cows had mating on their minds, Mama lost her cool at the innocent question. She lost no time in reporting the incident when back in the house, laughing so hard she could scarcely talk.

As hard as we worked, especially Mama and Daddy, there was also plenty of leisure time in the summer. Daddy would read and listen to baseball games on the radio, as we've seen. Or he'd strike out to go fishing, which involved long tours of the countryside.

Mama would go visiting, mostly. When I was little, June, Kay, Larry, and I would go with her to visit Miss Towne (teacher at Celt Elementary), Mrs. Fannie Early, and Miss Sally-Betty. We kids spent time hopping up and down the paved front walk toward the river, plunking at the old upright piano, checking out the large library above the winding closed-in stairs, and measuring our boredom by the ticking grandfather clock. After Mrs. Early died, in 1953 I think, we didn't visit so often, but Miss Towne visited us more, especially when her sister Inez was in from Cincinnati. The women sat out under the shade of the pear tree, Inez always refusing something to drink, saying, "I'm going to have a cold beer when I get home," which seemed to mortify Miss Towne.

About once a month or every six weeks or so we would walk the four or five miles over to Mama's homeplace and visit Brother Mac and family. But they came to our house more often. If we went through the fields by Uncle Ernest's house, we had to wade or hop across Whitelaw Snow's creek and Elijah Durrette's river.

We spent a fair amount of time each summer down at that river, usually accompanied by Mama and a bunch of the family kids. We went "swimming" in the muddy water to cool off on a mid-summer day. My three older brothers swam, but somehow Mama, afraid of water from almost drowning when a child, managed, irrationally, to dissuade Larry and me from learning to swim. After one of these wading and swimming episodes, I came out of the water to discover that my hand warts, two or three of them, were all gone. O holy waters, muddy as Jordan.

Mama liked to go to river baptisms, revivals, church lawn parties, all held in the summer—except for the lawn parties free, and sanctified entertainment to boot. Seeing full-dunk river baptisms led me even further along my decisive path of never joining the church. Such caterwauling as fat middle-aged women capped their being "saved" by being swept under the roiled-up, muddy water, to emerge with their clingy clothes, full dress usually, leaving very little to be imagined.

In my minimal religious life I had a sneaking fondness for each summer's Vacation Bible School. Somehow we got the two miles up the road to Amicus, where Jimmy Breeden's mother, living a couple of miles further, at the gas plant, picked us up and drove us to the church in Stanardsville right on Courthouse Square, Stanardsville Methodist. Larry and Jimmy Breeden inevitably fought with each other, but otherwise it was an edifying and peaceful week or two. I remember being best buddies with a boy there that I didn't otherwise know, Willis, seemingly more sophisticated than anyone I had known up to that time. He never turned up at William Monroe, so he was a mystery. I have since found out (thanks, Gayle Breeden Collier) that he was Willis Estes, first cousin of my best high school bud, Sanford Estes. Willis never came to Monroe because he lived just over the Orange County line.

When we went to the summer revival at Mt. Paran Methodist Church, we were not suspecting that the evangelist was in it for the swag and was about to abscond with the takings from several churches. What food for cynicism. And we had sung at every service "Heavenly Sunshine."

My first and nearly the only outdoor funeral service that I went to as a boy scarred me. In blistering heat, in July I think, I went with Mama to the burial of my Harlow first cousins' Uncle Jimmy Harlow, whom I did not know at all. Mama wanted someone to go with her, and perhaps I was the likeliest. The graveyard was up near the mountains somewhere. All of the congregation proceeded around the open coffin. I was knocked for a mental loop when I realized that I could smell the body in the coffin in the fierce heat. And then at the end of the service, my cousin Ethel worked herself up into a real crying frenzy and fainted dead away. I went to my Granddaddy McDaniel's funeral a few years later, and I think that was it for my youth.

My mother would certainly prefer a good funeral service to going to the movies. In fact, I don't recall either my mother or father ever going to a movie, though perhaps to a drive-in once. My earliest movie memory is vestigial, with no one now to confirm or negate the bits I have. I must have been four or five years old. The movie house seemed to be in Stanardsville, on the corner of Courthouse Square. However, I've never heard anyone else speak of a movie theater's ever having been in Stanardsville. If so, it closed down after a short while. Joe Clayson and Hazel took us, probably in 1948, and I remember that the movie was a western, with perhaps Gabby Hayes, with stagecoaches or one only going over a cliff, with a constant refrain of "Oh my darling Clementine" on the sound track. I'm almost certain that it was a B or lower movie, not Col. Sherman Potter's favorite, John Ford's classic *My Darling Clementine*. I remember being carried out of the theater by Joe, so I must have spent much of the time asleep.

Kay, Larry, and I saw many movies together in Charlottesville, and Larry and I only for the last few years of the fifties and early 1960.

Charlottesville, population then in the 20 thousands, had four movie houses—the elegant Paramount, the pretty-good Jefferson, and the seedy Lafayette downtown, and the University many blocks away, near the University of Virginia. We were often driven to town by one of our three older brothers working there then and left to progue the streets, Leggett's department store and Bargain Basement, Woolworth's, the Old Dominion bookstore, and movie houses, all day. They'd give us money for the day also. There we saw *Gone With the Wind,* apparently on its second septennial reissue, which would have been in 1953. *The Story of Ruth,* with its Israeli actress Elana Eden; *The Big Country,* with Gregory Peck, Jean Simmons, and Burl Ives; *Seven Brides for Seven Brothers;* and lots of African-set schlock, Biblical stories in the long run-up to *Ben-Hur,* and routine Hollywood fluff. We loved almost everything about the movies and went as often as we could, even for Joan Crawford's overacting eyebrows.

I remember the newsreels fondly enough. But the biggest eye-opener of all for me was a longish short of some great orchestra, perhaps the Philadelphia under Eugene Ormandy but I don't really remember. It may have been the first time I ever heard great swoops of meltingly beautiful classical music, borne away and enamored of it ever since. The whole screen other than the orchestra itself seemed to be lush red velvet or red carpeting, I know not in reality but in my memory so.

In those early years Hazel and Joe always came from Baltimore for the Fourth of July, for Joe loved fireworks and would then spend prodigally on them. We took the main show up to the grounds of Celt Elementary. Joe and my older brothers shot off the rockets, the cherry bombs, and the big-boom items, but we youngsters had little firecrackers with which to send tin cans aloft and sparklers, which we ran around the schoolhouse with, making as much commotion as possible. Alberta's family had a good view of the schoolhouse grounds from their house, a few hundred yards down the road, the only fireworks show to be had close around.

We made whistles of hollowed-out pulpy wood; we tied strings to the legs of June bugs and used them, cruelly, as if they were buzzing little kites; we skipped rocks on local streams; we ran across cow pastures, dodging the flops, looking out for killdeer nests on the ground; we ate every piece of wild fruit we could find. Rarely did we lack ways to keep busy, though Mama later told my wife that she had a hard time keeping me occupied.

Mama's interpretation was that I was too bright to maintain my interest in anything for very long at a time.

In the summer of 1958 or 1959, I don't remember which, Roy and I did most of the painting of the exterior of the homeplace for the first time. I suppose that he was on vacation, and I was on school's summer break. We had homemade scaffolds—supported by homemade triangles that rested against the house, with long poles in the corners of the triangles and in dug-in holes in the ground. The interior rooms had been painted many times by then. As is usual on such occasions, the workers always said self-effacingly, "It looks a lot better than it did."

The house as it looked painted, sometime in the 1960s.

When Hazel and Joe were home, when cousin Aubrey was there in Virginia for a long while, when my brother Fred had a pickup, our most constant pilgrimage was up the mountain to Shenandoah National Park, to drive along Skyline Drive, to visit the many caverns in the Shenandoah Valley, to stop at Big Meadows for a picnic, to walk down to Dark Hollow Falls. This was one trip that even Daddy was nearly always willing to take. He would pride himself on walking up to Byrd's Nest, and we younger kids would go with him.

We also visited everything we could having to do with Thomas Jefferson, Mr. Jefferson's Monticello and the University of Virginia being just 20-some miles away, in Charlottesville and near-Charlottesville.

I remember goggling at Edgar Allan Poe's room at the University and walking the Serpentine Wall and gazing up at the Rotunda. We also had James Monroe's Ash Lawn to visit, a very pleasant, less formal home than Monticello.

Pictures, taken mainly by brother-in-law Joe with his simple box cameras, abound from this period. There's usually a large group of us, sometimes traveling in two vehicles, Mama nearly always there, perhaps duded up in a homemade pastel suit, often with a hat on her head and a handbag, such as the light blue ostrich-skin one made by Aunt Dolly's husband, Armon Walton. I'm afraid that Larry and I are often in sandals with socks, our feet having grown unused to shoes since school let out. Larry and I nearly always look as pleased as well may be. Carl and Kay, for some reason, often look pensive. Niece Gail is there in picture after picture.

Sometimes we are decidedly less formal in pose. Oh, we stand facing the camera in clusters, but our clothes are askew and ill-buttoned. We have been to a river outing, perhaps a picnic, down near Fray's Store, Advance Mills. At night we saw the blinking red light on a tower atop the very low Fray's Mountain, which is near the little Charlottesville airport. As we listened to the radio in the dark, the blinking light was always there on the horizon, a la Gatsby. We passed by that tower on the way to the river abandon.

By mid-August the cicadas were whirring away every night, the whippoorwills repeating their call from up on the school grounds, the nights were growing cooler, and school would begin right after Labor Day (never beginning in August then). I looked forward to the new school year and began to get my things organized. Larry wanted to do just nothing to get ready. He wanted to spend more long days batting rocks into the air and running a whole fantasy sports league in his head.

Chapter 9

Specimen Days: Fall and Winter

As spring peepers heralded all of the green excess to come in April and, further along, all of the "blazing circumstance" (Richard Wilbur) of summer, the turning and re-turning of the seasons, so cicadas chirred the end of August and summer's glut. Right after Labor Day, the new school year would begin, the semester then lapping over into January.

Come September in Piedmont Virginia, the days are very warm and the nights sometimes chilly. To go out into the dew early in the morning, as we extended the barefoot season as far as we could, was to admit that parents are sometimes right: time to put on shoes again. We couldn't go to William Monroe without shoes anyway.

But as soon as we got home from our school day, Larry and I shucked our shoes, grabbed a snack, and padded down the dirt road on our way to Uncle Ernest's. We went there mainly to read the *Washington Post,* the *Times-Herald* in the early days. In woven-twine-bottomed chairs we sat side by side and spread out the full-size newspaper on the edge of Uncle Ernest and Aunt Ruby's chenille-covered bed. The room was not just their bedroom but one of the two heated rooms in the house, doubling as a living room, and TV room from about 1952 or '53 on. We read the paper back to front, starting with the *Post*'s generous spread of four or five pages of comics.

We read essentially all of the comics, sometimes giving but slight attention to World War II remnants like "Buzz Sawyer" and "Steve Canyon," liking the latter better once Poteet was introduced. Some strips we gave short shrift, like the insufferable "Little Orphan Annie," the unfunny "Nancy," and the mostly pointless "Henry." We liked "Steve Roper" especially after Mike Nomad entered, along with Ma Jong, his landlady. We were fond of "Little Lulu" and the strip's Witch Hazel, of "Blondie," of "Our Boarding House," with Maj. Amos B. Hoople uttering "Fap!" to Martha's backing up a dictum with her rolling pin. "Bringing Up Father" we called "Maggie and Jiggs," of course, and sided with Jiggs against her love of opera and hatred of corned beef and cabbage. "L'il Abner" was a cultural institution, and our sisters talked of Schmoos, Sadie Hawkins Day, Mammy Yokum, and Daisy Mae as if they were well-known neighbors and events. This was before Al Capp gave up pure comedy for becoming a right-wing culture warrior.

"Dick Tracy" gave us an endless supply of villains and creeptoids, June especially relishing B. O. Plenty and Gravel Gertie. Her favorite comic strip was probably "Brenda Starr, Reporter" with Basil, her Mystery Man seeking a cure for his ineffable, mystery disorder. We boys weren't ashamed of reading the soap-opera, girly strips like "Mary Worth," "Rex Morgan, M. D.," and "Apartment 3-G," but we never talked about them either.

Easily my favorite then, an all-time favorite still, was Walt Kelly's "Pogo" with its lovely line drawings of the Okefenokee Swamp, its inventive word-play, its inspired nonsense like "Deck us all with Boston Charlie," its caricatures of political figures like Joe McCarthy, Nikita Khrushchev, and J. Edgar Hoover, and its huge cast of anthropomorphic "animules"—the gentle Pogo Possum, science-mad quack Howland Owl (howl and howl), Churchy LaFemme (who got "turtler and turtler every year"), Albert Alligorator ("A handsome man looks good in anything he throw on his back."), and the wonderfully diverse, wacky cosmos of more memorable characters than a dozen other comic strips: Deacon Mushrat, flirting with McCarthyism in Gothic-lettered sonorities; the Eeyorish Porky Pine; Sarcophagus MacAbre, a buzzard; Miss Mam'selle Hepzibah, the Frenglish-speaking skunk with a Hebraic name; Beauregard, lover of DOGgerel; Pup-Dog, the cutest cartoon puppy of all time; con-animals like P. T. Bridgeport and Seminole Sam, the fox; the hectoring hen with megaphone, Miss Sis Boombah; Snavely Snake, who would lose falls to the

Worm-chile; Fremont Beetle; Tammananny Tiger; Miz Beaver, with her corncob pipe; the Commie cowbirds; Rackety Coon and Bun Rabbit; the great linguist who never used a vowel, Grundoon Groundhog; and a trio of my absolute favorites, the bats Bewitched, Bothered, and Bemildred [love those names], doing comic shtick richer than "Who's on First?"

On the comics pages, we did—mostly in our head, in case Uncle Ernest would want them later—the Wishing Well, word jumbles, and bits of the crossword puzzle. When we got to the sports section, Larry, wanting more detail than I did on things like box scores, would sometimes stall while I moved on, pausing on the editorial page always for at least the cartoons of the great Herblock. Much of our knowledge of the world then came from this newspaper perusal.

The newspaper semi-digested a day before it went to Daddy the next morning, we would often watch a bit of late afternoon television, but only if it was offered. Aunt Ruby usually had us do some chore first, such as carrying buckets of water up the steep hill from their spring, or gathering yet another box of chips for fire-starting, joining the dozens of other boxes in their downstairs backroom. Then she'd say, "You can turn on, and [giggling] later on in life you can turn out."

We mostly sneered at the children's shows on that time of day, such as "Howdy Doody," though we made a little exception for some of Pinky Lee and for the continuing stories on "The Mickey Mouse Club." Mostly we saw old westerns with the likes of Hoot Gibson, Lash Larue, Bob Steele, and Ken Maynard—old, inferior movie shorts from the 1930s and 1940s.

I found October, most of it, to be the most engaging month of the year. I may have been a bit prejudiced, since my birthday was October 3, and I felt like I had some ownership in the month. We mostly had very mild and sunny weather. Living near the foot of the Blue Ridge Mountains, we saw glorious colors, both of fall foliage and sunsets. To the north and west, the sky often dazzled, the woods a riot of tulip poplar yellow, the crimsons of maples, and the dark reds of dogwoods—Virginia's state flower, peppering our woods all over. Near the house, cardinals—Virginia's state bird—and black-capped chickadees grew more numerous. We had seen the V-wedges of migratory birds going south, and starlings sometimes massed in armies, undulating in waves against the blue background.

As fall crept on and began to threaten earnest change, we growing boys had responsibilities. When I was about five, I didn't need to worry about firewood. It was a lark to ride on Uncle Ernest's wagon with pole standards over to our wood to get lengths of polewood to be sawn by the older boys, before we used anything but bowsaws and crosscuts—no speedy chainsaws then for us. Once when the wagon approached our house for unloading, I hoped to beat Larry and Kay to the house, jumping off the wagon to cut across a harvested corn field. I tripped on a corn stalk that had been cut off at an angle close to the ground and landed face down on another. Blood was gushing, some of it getting into my eye as I ran squawling to Mama. I probably should have had stitches, but, as always, we made do with home care. To this day, I carry a worm-shaped scar beside my mouth on the right side, the source of queries, ever after, about what happened.

On a happier note, once or twice when I was a young boy hanging out with Uncle Ernest hauling wood, he let me ride one of the two big farm horses for a short distance. I can't remember whether I sat on Maud or Nell, but I remember Uncle Ernest's teaching me the difference between "Gee" and "Haw" according to which direction I wanted the mare to turn. I could scarcely curve my legs around the very large horse under me. Since the horse was hitched to a wagon she had no saddle on, so I held tight to whatever I could. On another occasion, as we were going down the rubble-rock road to Uncle Ernest's flat to haul back feed corn, I was put in charge of holding the brake on the wagon. Heady powers!

Within a few years, Larry and I were cutting wood for a while every afternoon after getting home from school, mostly with a shared bowsaw. Daddy did most of the splitting of wood, the big pieces for the heaters, though we did a bit in the later years of high school. Cutting, splitting, stacking, later toting the wood to a woodshed, and dashing out in our shirtsleeves to get a "turn" of wood—the local locution—to feed the insatiable fires was "boys' work," just as doing the dishes and helping with washing clothes and ironing was "girls' work."

The cookstove, a pretty light green and cream one in my early days, was kept going all day long and into the night in cold weather. It devoured sto'wood. It had a damper to regulate the burn, but Mama mostly wanted the oven hot for biscuits, cornbread, and pies. The fire lay in a narrow, long grate beneath only the first two circular stovelids (with connecting ironwork). The smoke and much of the heat flowed to the right, over the top of the oven, to the stovepipe sealed in the flue. So the next four stovelids gave the cook ever-modulating heat for simmering foods and separating the curds and whey in clabber milk. On the far right was a large water tank that could bring water not to the boiling point but at least up to the temperatures usual in water heaters. On a raised section—the stove's back, at right angles to the cook surface—was a double-doored warming oven, always called "the warming closet" in our household, which as a very small boy, trying to make sense of a fresh world, I heard as "woman closet." Here, leftover bread, rice pudding, or corn on the cob could be kept warm and soft.

The ashes from the spent wood dropped through the grate to an ashbox below, and there was a cleanout also, wherein Mama wielded the sootrake, a rectangular piece of metal welded to a long metal handle. When the ashbox was full, it was pulled out and dumped wherever. Mama always said that the wood ashes would make bluegrass grow. She was right at least to the extent that bluegrass likes a lower pH than most grasses.

We boys kept the woodboxes supplied, though Daddy would often carry the great fat lengths of heater wood in to supply the long, narrow heater in Mama and Daddy's bedroom. When there was a dining room separate from the kitchen, in early years and later years but not the middle years, the dining room doubled as a living room and was also heated, with a "Warm Morning" type of heater. (The dining room was the largest room in the house.) The black cast iron box, much larger than the bedroom heater's burn box, was surrounded by a cosmetically more appealing brown enamel box that one could lean against and warm one's butt. Uncle Ernest sometimes burned a bit of coal, but we were strictly wood-burners.

If the heaters, the large dining room one especially, were carefully damped, a bit of fire might be shepherded through the night so that the stove was easy to get going the next morning. The cookstove, of course, had to be restarted each morning. Mama used a bit of kerosene to start the fire, out of favor these days. Kerosene was kept in a used gallon cider vinegar jug. It was Mama's sovereign remedy for any little cut, scratch, or rash. It smelled vile, but I have to admit that it worked well for speeding up the healing of small wounds.

Once there was room enough for me upstairs with my siblings, we all slept up there in unheated rooms. Oh, they were hot, hot, hot on summer nights, with only a small attic above and no insulation, but equally frigid on cold winter nights, even with some heat from below and from the flue in the bedroom above Mama and Daddy's, Larry's and mine late in the '50s. On really cold nights Mama would wrap a heated brick in a towel for us to put in the bottom of the bed, but going to bed meant that we curled up into a fetal position and gradually unfurled as the weighty quilts and blankets above us held in the heat we generated. But what good sleeping! We were usually in bed sometime between 9 and 10 p.m. and jumped out of bed at 7 a.m. and ran to finish dressing at the downstairs stoves. Older brothers and sisters, used to central heating, made an excessively big deal of the cold when they came home in winter, and we chaffed them for growing soft.

Sometimes while we boys worked on the woodpile, June and Kay (Hazel and Violet long ago gone out into the world) were working on dishes. We had no sink or piped-in water until later, so with the buckets of water that the boys had toted from the spring, now heated in the water tank or in large cast-iron tea kettles, the girls washed, drained, and dried the dishes. Usually the same sorts of soaps used for laundry were used for dishes. The dishpan was enameled, about 18 inches in diameter; the dish drain was a large rectangular bread pan. Dishes were rarely rinsed, so I suppose we ingested minute quantities of soap over the years. Mama's favorite frying pan was a 12-inch cast iron one with the handle now broken off, which huge pan full of hot liquid I saw Mama, this 4-foot, 11-inch woman, sometimes heft one-handed with the thinnest of pot-holders for cushion. She loved cast-iron, as do I, but her cast-iron was always washed in soapy water, and so it was not properly seasoned thereafter and was clearly not nonstick. June grew so weary of washing stuck-up dishes and pots and pans that she vowed that later on in life she was using only disposables.

When I was four and five years old and beyond, Mama, June, and Kay used "sad irons," heavy cast-iron implements, maybe a half dozen of them kept in constant rotation heating on the stoves, to iron most of the clothes we wore. This was well before the days of "permanent press," and most of the clothes we wore were cotton or wool. It was considered indecent to go away from home in unironed clothes. Especially in fall and winter, we were usually well turned out in the clothes we had. We did not have a great variety, but what we had were well cared for. Mama was in her early forties then and indefatigable in her labors. She also had a bit of professional pride to bolster her up: for a short while she had worked in a laundry in Baltimore, adding $7 a week (!) to the family coffers. Home laundry in the late 1940s and early 1950s still involved a lot of bleaching, blueing, and dipping of clothes into starch water and hand wringing them. Men's dress shirts, especially, were quite demanding. And Mama could remember when Daddy was something of a dandy, wearing silk dress shirts at $30 a pop, a huge chunk of change in the 1920s.

On laundry and ironing days in the fall and winter the house was fragrant and steamy. The wash tubs had water as hot as hands could stand it, the clothes dipped out with a stick, fragrant with homemade lye soap, bars of Octagon, and detergents like Oxydol. In dishpans and large bowls, whites like dress shirts were getting blued and frilly items getting starched, all with their characteristic odors. The sprinkled damp clothes gave up their moisture in steam as the irons thumped and glided. On the stove a big cast-iron tea kettle poured out steam in accompaniment to the hissing sad irons.

Perhaps when I was six or seven, Mama got an electric iron, no doubt a present from Hazel or Violet, remembering the hard duty of the sad irons. I was not very old when Mama showed me the professional way to iron a shirt, starting with the back yoke. I was interested, quite unembarrassed (as long as Daddy wasn't around), and have used the knowledge now for 60-odd years.

In late September chinquapins ripened, and our long season of wild nut-gathering began—first these small chestnuts with the Indian name, and then in October hazelnuts and hickory nuts, the shagbark ones the best, and on into November to finish up the black walnuts and butternuts. The antiquated sad irons, set between our legs with the bottom up, now did duty as a surface on which to crack nuts indoors, unless we preferred firewood.

Scarcely anyone has drawn the change that comes this time of year so well as the medieval "Pearl Poet" in *Sir Gawain and the Green Knight*. As Theodore H. Banks, Jr., translates this Middle English work, this is what happens:

The leaves from the limbs drop, and light on the ground;

And withers the grass that grew once so greenly.

Then all ripens that formerly flourished, and rots;

And thus passes the year in yesterdays many . . . .

The year indeed passed in yesterdays many. The region where I lived cinched its belt and soldiered on. By September the garden was mostly spent. Mama was still making green tomato ketchup—a relish really—with the last of those. Turnips had been sown where the potatoes had been dug. The fodder had been cut and stowed in the barn to help the cows through the winter. Milk production was tapering off, and our diet changed accordingly. Now dried beans (the musical fruit), grain, and canned goods dominated the diet, fresh pork yet to come. Frost threatened fairly often in September but rarely came until well into October. By November Daddy didn't have so much to do outdoors and usually set to refurbishing our kitchen and dining room chairs, renewing or replacing axe handles and garden implements, and readying for the big event of hog-butchering.

Every few years Daddy had to re-bottom some of our chairs, the simple, inexpensive kitchen-type chairs that must have originally had seats of woven caning. He replaced the bottoms with woven twine, regular yellowish-brown hay-baling twine. He was rather good at the chore, being more artistic than he was in most things. Usually he wove in a regular cross-hatch pattern, going over and under every three to five strands of the twine. A long piece of wire from a coathanger was his shuttle, and all knots were made on the underside of the seat. Occasionally he would do a fancy artistic pattern of more intricate design. A twine-bottomed chair is a little prickly when the twine is brand-new, but human backsides wore away the irradiating threads quickly. A new twine seat soon relaxed and gave a little, making a comfortable chair bottom. The backs of these chairs were always curved and slightly inclined, good sitting indeed, so long as you didn't want to lean your head if you were a grownup. With these chairs and a long, backless bench against the wall, our dining table would easily seat a dozen people if some were small.

The big table, chairs, bench, and two "safes" made up most of the dining room furniture. One safe was where everyday dishes, cutlery, and leftover food were kept. Most people would call it a "pie safe," its perforated tin panels dominating the top part of the cabinet. The other safe had a glass door, intended to be more upscale, though it looked rough enough with its accumulated clutter. Here sat some of Mama's best dishes, a few cut-glass bowls for serving fruit to go with homemade cakes and the cake plates and stands—a flat amber Depression ware plate or two and also clear fancy glass raised cake stands. Here also were displayed green Depression ware dessert dishes and pretty blue salt and pepper shakers apparently made of Bakelite.

With cooler and colder weather we listened to the radio for longer hours, especially before we had a television at Uncle Ernest's. Even post-TV we rarely went over to Uncle Ernest's more than twice a week at night. We called dibs: "I'm sitting at the radio tonight." Then we got to choose the programs. The radio, a good wooden one with good, deep sound, for a long while had a loose connection of some kind. So we laid a wood-handled butcher knife under the volume and the tuning knobs. The pressure kept the connection as the radio sat on the corner of the big dining table. If we had homework, we did it as we listened to the radio. Back then we kids all had more than a one-track mind, and homework wasn't all that hard.

Pre-1956 and our enrapturement with rock and roll, early in the night we listened mostly to WCKY in Cincinnati, to "Suppertime Frolic," country music when it had not become a subset of pop music, before Nashvillization. Sometimes we followed that with "Polka Party," of all things for country kids to listen to. But we mostly relished comedy programs at regular times: "Our Miss Brooks," with the delightful Eve Arden and Richard Crenna; "Jack Benny"; "Amos and Andy"; and "George Burns and Gracie Allen." Benny, Burns and Allen, and Miss Brooks all translated to television just fine. Indeed Burns and Allen may have been my favorite comedy on television of all the many programs we watched. I know of no finer comedienne than Gracie, with her deadpan, insouciant non sequiturs and light touch.

Before the spring of 1956, when Kay graduated from high school and went to Baltimore to start work as a monotypist at a medical publishing company, she, Larry, and I would go over to Uncle Ernest and Aunt Ruby's house about twice a week, toting a kerosene lantern or flashlights, to watch television for about two hours. On clear nights with a full or nearly full moon we navigated the one-fourth mile or more quite easily without any artificial lights, down the gravel road, through the woods to the gate, and through the field by the cedar and sycamore trees. Above, more stars than I have ever seen since, with NO light pollution, and the Milky Way gave enough light on dazzlingly clear winter nights. At the beginning we were feeling our way around the new country of tobbabiggen (as Larry and I, who sometimes spoke an almost, private language between just ourselves, called it after a while). We tried and experimented with which nights to watch. Since we had only two stations to choose from, WSVA in Harrisonburg and WTVR in Richmond, and occasionally a very shadowy, ghostly Lynchburg station, we soon settled on our favorites that would also please Uncle Ernest. Aunt Ruby didn't seem to get much engaged in the programs.

I can remember snippets featuring early TV personalities, some of them very New Yorkerish—Dagmar, the Goldbergs—and others like "I Remember Mama" and "Kukla, Fran, and Ollie." Early on, however, we settled on one-hour comedy/variety programs that both generations enjoyed, our first choice being "The Colgate Comedy Hour," often with Dean Martin and Jerry Lewis or the wacky, over-the-top comedy of Martha Raye. There we saw more and more of popular singers like Jo Stafford and light opera singers. On Sunday night Uncle Ernest always wanted to watch the Ed Sullivan Show, and so we did. I remember best Julie Andrews and Richard Burton doing numbers from the Broadway *Camelot*. Our favorites were mostly half-hour comedy shows, such as "Topper" and Ann Sothern's "Private Secretary" or "My Little Margie," with Gale Storm. And of course Jack Benny and Burns and Allen. One of Uncle Ernest's favorites, Jackie Gleason, I never liked, on the whole, though Art Carney was always irresistible, as was Audrey Meadows. Inevitably, we also saw "I Love Lucy."

I remember some longer, serialized programs, the best I recall being "When Knighthood Was in Flower," with Richard Todd and the winning, gravel-voiced Glynis Johns. Richard Todd also, as I remember, did a mighty fine Robin Hood. I think we had Walt Disney to thank for both series. This was also the beginning of the big craze for Westerns. For Larry and me, after Kay left, it was the time for "Maverick," with the charming James Garner as Bret and, less so, Jack Kelly as his cousin Bart; "Cheyenne," with big Clint Walker; and the self-effacing Will Hutchins as "Sugarfoot," all three of which westerns appealed to us a good deal more than the more serious westerns such as "Gunsmoke."

A big part of our youth was being over at Uncle Ernest and Aunt Ruby's house at night. I don't remember ever being served any food. Aunt

Ruby didn't much like cooking at that time in her life, and the kitchen had long ago gone cold. Anyway, we were likely to have started out from home with our hands stuffed with food. Uncle Ernest was at his corniest then, lying on a sideless scroll-end black chaise longue, I guess you'd call it, chewing tobacco as he read the newspaper, frequently raising the newspaper up so that he could check out what was happening on TV, commenting. Occasionally, he'd make a slightly obscene joke about the goings-on, especially if just Larry and I were there. For a time cousin Aubrey was there too in the late '50s, and he egged Uncle Ernest on. On bitter cold nights Uncle Ernest sometimes went out by lantern light to tend to new piglets or some other farm animals.

The room was neat, neater than anything at home, but also kitschier. Above the TV was an electric clock in the form of a black-and-white cat with rolling eyes and a switching tail like a metronome. On the left wall was a wooden crescent moon with steps to be used as bric-a-brac shelves. On a cluttered dresser sat the usual gear, with good hair brushes. Uncle Ernest was rather vain of his silvery hair neatly brushed. In a canister were numerous cigarettes, I suppose for company, since I didn't see Uncle Ernest smoke. I was humiliated on one occasion when I decided to affect a playboy pose with cigarette dangling from my lips. I was alone in the room striking Hollywood poses but glanced up to see Uncle Ernest gazing at me through the window, having come from milking to ask Aunt Ruby something. I was mortified, probably worse because Uncle Ernest never said a word; but I never smoked even for two seconds after this embarrassment.

On Saturday mornings Larry and I would go to read the Washington newspaper, and, especially if it was foul out, with slushy melting snow, we would be lured into watching "Super Circus," for Leo Fenner, Maude Walton's Oregonian husband, was often there by himself and thought Mary Hartline, the leader of the band, in cowgirl boots, tassels, and platinum blonde hair, the hottest babe on television. Though she is often called "television's first sex symbol," Larry and I found her not just silly but not appealing, with bad legs. Still, we watched the trash, and felt bad when we got back out into the sun and melting snow, with the beginnings of a headache and black dots before our eyes.

In the 1950s PBS was a good way into the future (1970), and television advertising, not to say hucksterism, was young, relatively unrestrained, long-winded, and egregious. Perhaps there were no more minutes of ads in prime-time than today—I don't really know—but most programs, instead of running many 15-second ads not related to the show, had one or two sponsors only, running ads that seemed to go on and on. For instance, the program would be paid for by Chrysler automobiles, Westinghouse appliances, or Old Gold cigarettes. Consequently, the ads would go on for a full two minutes, a spokesperson trumpeting the merits of the product, minor celebrities like Betty Furness for Westinghouse, the ubiquitous Dennis James for Old Gold cigarettes, or the equally ubiquitous John Cameron Swayze for whatever, not just Timex watches.

A television advertising case unto itself was the hawking of Geritol, a tonic for "iron-poor tired blood," with "twice the iron in a pound of calf's liver." Left out of the advertising was this outstanding fact: the tonic was 24 proof (12% alcohol). By the end of the decade Geritol was brought up short for false and misleading advertising, and it transmuted into a now-respectable, I assume, line of vitamin supplements. But we were hammered over and over with those ads, adding another, lesser phrase to the British "bone idle"— "tired blood."

A similar case was that of Hadacol, which we heard advertised constantly on the radio and saw in print. First concocted by a U. S. senator from Louisiana, it was sold as a "dietary supplement" also, containing B-complex vitamins and, again, was 24 proof. I suppose the -ol ending is a slight clue, but Hadacol listed the alcohol as a "preservative." This snake oil did especially well in the dry Southern states in the early '50s. It is reported that it was sold in New Orleans bars in shot glasses. Finally it ran afoul of the law just as Geritol had, but we knew what kind of world we were living in when Madmen (Madison Avenue hucksters and wannabes) made money from the gullible while perhaps endangering their health.

The Madison Avenue creations for the print media, especially for magazines and in-store posters, would sometimes look startling to today's eyes—not the gentle stuff like Joan Caulfield gushing over Royal Crown Cola, I think it was, but surely by Risë Stevens, an opera star, advertising Camel cigarettes, with an outline T drawn over her nose, mouth, and throat, signifying the "taste zone." Wonder what Camels did to her voice, to the "V-zone."

By the latter part of November, usually somewhat close to Thanksgiving, it was continuously cold enough to kill hogs for the winter. Squeamish children—and Larry and I were either excessively squeamish or excessively sensitive—found this time to be quite trying. We saw the preparations, and as much as we liked pork—the readiest supply of meat and often the only meat we had—we hated to see the lead-in preparations. I probably didn't know the word "ambivalent" then, but this was the very essence of ambivalence. Just as there was usually but one copper apple butter kettle in a sizable community, passed around from one family to another in the true communal spirit, so there would be but one large scalding pan in the community. When Daddy had dug out a big trench close to the stream that ran below our spring and through the pig pen, big enough trench to hold a sizable fire under the pan, and when the pan had been filled with tens of buckets of water from the spring, when the fire had been blazing for hours since earliest morning and the water was steaming hot, the process began.

These were pigs that we had helped slop and given treats to. We didn't give them names as we did our cows, but still they were smart and personable creatures. Though the pig pen was two hundred yards or so away from the house and we were closed up inside with something over our ears, we could still hear the shots and the squealing. We would sometimes sing or shout nonsense incantations to blot out the noise.

Still, once the (usually) five pigs were clearly dead and ready for the scalding pan, the processes of butchering were easier to take. I don't know how, exactly, the huge pigs were maneuvered briefly into the scalding pan, though of course it relied on sheer manpower, neighbors always helping each other in numbers. The scalding was necessary to get rid of the bristles, scraped off with knives and zinc canning jar screw-ons then. We ate the bacon, for instance, with the skin, pork rind, still on.

The carcasses of the pigs were then hauled up near to the meat house, with sturdy wood lengths stuck through the trotters so that the pigs could be hung upside down, the wood supports hung over one-large-ended S-hooks hung to a big wooden frame like a heavy duty swing support. The men expertly cut the meat into hams, shoulders, side bacon, and so on, just about everything being used, including the feet. Mama and Oscar Steppe would clean the "chitlins," and mostly the assembled women and larger children would begin the greasy work of cutting the fatter parts of the meat into chunks to be rendered into lard and cracklin' remains from the lard-making.

The work took essentially all day, no matter how many hands were involved. The community help would go away with some fresh pork to cook, probably for supper that night, and the benison thus rotated through the whole community along with the scalding pan. By night-time—and we worked well into the night on such occasions, by blazing fires under the cast-iron wash pot, by makeshift torcheres of oily, tightly wrapped cloth, by kerosene lanterns—we had heavily salted, peppered, and sometimes brown-sugared hams for Christmas and Easter, shoulders for boiling or for frying slices of, huge slabs of side meat for bacon, jowl meat for cooking with black-eyed peas on New Year's day, and chunks of salt port, streak-of-lean, for seasoning greens and dried beans. It went into the cavernous big-slabbed meatbox in the meathouse, and the door was locked. Come what may, we would have meat once a day anyway, to help fuel us through the drear winter. We would have sausage gravy, fried tenderloin, un-nitrated bacon, and fresh Virginia ham, and so we endured the grim work of butchery.

Outside in the dark partly illumed with time-old blazes, a scene that might have been lifted from a novel by Thomas Hardy, the hard, dirty, and greasy work had been but preparation for the festive night. Mama's work was still not done—the sausage to be ground, seasoned, and canned; excess tenderloins to be canned—but we had fried fresh tenderloin for supper, probably with home fries with onions, and something like green beans, and some sort of dessert—in other words, a hot, full dinner for supper.

For whatever reason, Thanksgiving day was much less a holiday than hog-killing day. We never had turkey, and I don't remember ever hearing a thanksgiving prayer at mealtime on that or any other day except when Mama's preacher came for dinner. I suppose we were thankful, just in the mute or inarticulate heathen manner. It was a shock to my system when I went away to Emory and Henry College to see many students saying a silent grace before every meal. Of course, pious souls, especially teenagers, must be allowed some rebellion. I sometimes heard uttered prayers like "God is great, God is good: I'm impressed!"

Once Thanksgiving was past—and there was no Black Friday

then—the merchandising and Tin Pan Alleyizing of Christmas could slowly begin. Can you imagine such a time?

In school at Celt Elementary, we started learning and practicing some traditional (that is to say, from the nineteenth century) Christmas songs for our annual holiday celebration: "Away in the Manger," "O Little Town of Bethlehem," "Hark! the Herald Angels," and "It Came Upon a Midnight Clear." So far as I remember, we practiced almost altogether religious-themed Christmas songs. As when we had monthly Bible teacher visits, nobody paid any attention to the separation of church and state in our schools.

Still, Christmas was most in our ears and on our minds from listening to the radio. It was the big heyday of secular Christmas songs that are now classics. From earlier years than mine, Bing Crosby already epitomized pop Christmas songs, with Perry Como no small contributor. Newer performances, especially from Jimmy Wakely and Margaret Whiting ("Silver Bells"), "Winter Wonderland," "Rudolph, the Red-Nosed Reindeer" (gorblimey, old Gene Autry), and Santa Claus songs that really spoke to Larry and me when young, such as "Here Comes Santa Claus" and "Up on the House-Top"—all of these filled the air waves, with the late-50s contributions of rock performers such as Brenda Lee and Bobby Helms added to the brew.

Larry and I clung to our belief in Santa long after we should have known better, partly because smart-ass Kenny Marshall had insisted from way back in elementary school "It's your mama and daddy." We didn't want to give him the satisfaction of believing him. We set out a shoebox for Santa, mantels and stockings being no part of our tradition. It was filled mainly with candy, nuts, oranges, and the old loose-skinned Dancy tangerines, with a few small toys. Having much older siblings was a great advantage, for Hazel, and maybe Violet added in, gave us a really neat train set, not plug-in electric but with a wind-up locomotive, I think, that clanged and gave off sparks as it pulled a number of cars around the oval track. Later, Fred gave us a bicycle for Christmas—one between the two of us—a nice red and white one with streamers.

We never got a tree until a week before Christmas, one we cut on our own land and immediately put into a milk crock with water and rocks to hold it steady. Most of the time the tree was cedar but occasionally a white pine or a hemlock, the hemlock poached from Whitelaw Snow's woods, for we had none. No electric lights for us—only glass ornaments, garlands, icicles, candy canes, and things of that sort. The tree usually came down on New Year's day but occasionally stayed up until twelfth-night.

Someone or ones, probably mainly older children out working, went quite overboard on Christmas treats: the house was usually overflowing with candy—bon bons, chocolate drops, "French" candy, lots of filled candy and ribbons and other hard candy of all sorts with several boxes of Whitman's Sampler chocolates—with oranges, tangerines, and sometimes grapefruit, and with nuts in shells, nuts galore—almonds, filberts, pecans, English walnuts, and Brazil nuts. Mama made several cakes; we had all sorts of canned fruits and pickles; we had a huge boiled ham to eat especially with eggs at breakfast but to piece on until nothing was left except the bone and some shreds of fat for the dogs and cats.

In my youth there were three dogs and numerous cats at home. The dogs were Fred's hunting dog, Rover, a whitish low-slung dog, fierce on rabbits and squirrels; Carl's dog, Spot, I suppose mainly a hound, also a hunting dog; and the general dog Snowball, a white Spitz that didn't seem to do anything but act slightly deranged. They were just there, harmless and friendly, but somehow dogs just never appealed to me. In the very early days Fred and Carl had a rescue tuxedo cat that they called Monroe. I may remember correctly in thinking that they had found it near our high school, William Monroe in Stanardsville. But the calico cat Fluffy was the materfamilias of lots of very winning kittens. Mama fed the cats, mainly milk from the cows and raw biscuit dough which they begged from her. One begging cat with something wrong with his tail got stepped on by Mama at work in the kitchen. The tail came right off! However, the cat thrived thereafter, perhaps his health improved. Later, we had a family of tailless Manx cats, but I don't know where they came from. The cats got meat scraps and were expected to hunt mice and other critters. When Daddy contemplated getting rid of all of the cats, the mice in the barn were sufficient argument even for his stubbornness. The cats, in the way of the world, caught lots of critters, even occasionally killing snakes of size. The dogs seemed to believe in peaceful co-existence with snakes.

It was wild country, and we rambled everywhere, encountering far more snakes than I ever have since. Most of them were black snakes or other harmless ones, but we saw an occasional copperhead. And the trouble with black snakes is that they seemed to delight in catching kids off guard, coiling around at one's feet when one was driving cows through the woods, or lying on the sill of the springhouse, spotted only when one had to go back out. Mama took black snakes to be her mortal enemies regardless of what we told her from our book l'arning. But late fall and winter were relished for being snake-free.

Having snow for Christmas was not common at all but not totally unknown either. We didn't get enough snow in my youth, but we had some deep ones and even missed school because of snow on fairly rare occasions. The barn hill was an excellent one for sledding, long and fairly gentle. If we wanted real dare-deviltry, we went over the hill above our spring to go down the very steep and shorter hill down toward an older spring. We had one regular sto'-bought sled with metal rails and twist-bar steering. In Roy's heyday we also had heavier and unsteerable sleds cobbled together from spare planks. They would go fast but usually landed one in the boggy land next to the stream from our spring.

We wore galoshes, as we had to wear to school for very bad weather, the main problem being that the galoshes were usually too small to allow wearing them with warm shoes inside and too large to be fully fitting even with several pairs of old socks on. Before the days of downy, padded winter wear, we usually got too cold after about a half hour on the slopes and went inside wanting cocoa made from scratch. Of course we built snow forts and aimed to maim each other with icy snowballs.

Uncle Ernest seemed to be in his element when it snowed. He hitched Maud and Nell to a homemade big V-shaped sledge and plowed out the road to his house, plowed up the gravel road to our house, and perhaps plowed the rough road over to Dan Collier's. He told me what I didn't know beforehand—to always wear a warm cap or hat on the head since a large percentage of the body's heat is lost through the head. Still, he did not scruple to have fun with our winter wear: I had a favorite long winter coat, sort of white, that I wore when very small. Uncle Ernest laughed every time he saw it and said, "I see you've got your duster on." Somewhere he had picked up that English term and relished tossing it at me every chance he got. The next winter I was distressed to discover that Mama had gotten rid of my favorite coat without asking or telling me. It was probably outgrown, but it was dear enough to me for me to brave Uncle Ernest's badinage.

One warm, sunny January day, bored with winter cabin fever, Larry and I rambled down to Elijah Durrette/Frank Durrette's (the old man now dead for years) river bottomland, further upstream than we usually prowled in warm seasons. It must have been steadily cold, though not arctically or we would have noted, for a fairly long period, for we found a section of the river with little vegetation on the banks and saw ice, obviously thick and solid, from bank to bank. As the saying goes, our mama didn't raise no fools, so we found a number of big rocks, as big as we could tote, and heaved them down onto the surface of the ice. Nothing but the tiniest of dents and ice slivers, so it would obviously hold two skinny boys. There was no snow on the ground, so we cleared off the rocks we had tested the rink with and started running and then free sliding on the surface of the river, for dozens of yards per run. We kept at it for an hour or two, no doubt the best winter games, the best Olympics, we had ever had. I don't remember whether we ever told Mama of our venture, for she was mighty peculiar about such things, even if she could see that we were perfectly safe.

Mama was usually quite gentle and patient, the opposite of Daddy, but it must be admitted that with Larry and me, the two youngest, she was far more likely to punish us, usually making us go cut our own switches from a sour cherry tree or a lilac bush. She whipped only around the ankles. Winter must have tested her, for we were in the house more than usual, ornery and sometimes bored. My most vivid memory of Mama the Avenger was the Cocoa Episode. Larry and I kept bubbling our cocoa, blowing bubbles over the surface and just generally making a silly mess. She warned us a couple of times, and then we could see that she was in earnest, her nerves probably frayed. We slid off our chairs and went under the table. But Mama was mad enough, and young enough, that she caught both of us, by the hair, I think, and dragged us out. Then we got a Mama-drubbing. The indignity and embarrassment were worse than the punishment.

Though Daddy would punish us with his mouth, I remember just one occasion in the 16-plus years that I lived at home as a kid that he tried physical punishment on Larry and me. Mama was not at home, and I don't remember what occasioned the blow-up, but I'm sure that Larry and

I had just been "showing our asses," as the salty regionalism has it. Daddy hauled the two of outside the kitchen door and stripped off his belt. Daddy always wore his pants low-slung and seemed to lack the usual issuance of hips; we feared that his pants would fall right down. Somehow, Larry and I perceived that Daddy was a rank amateur at this little-boy chastising bit. We squirmed and giggled so that he could make no progress in punishing us. He gave up in quick exasperation, beating us with his tongue as he retreated. Larry and I sat there in a heap and wondered at how so frank-talking a daddy couldn't do this job with any sort of credit.

We went outdoors in all weathers, and winter necessitated some inventiveness to keep amused. Huge daggers of icicles hung from the house eaves rather often. Of course, this required us to throw a tennis ball at them, time after time, trying to get the daggers to spike into the ground essentially unharmed. If that failed, we still had the fun of smashing things and hearing all of the interesting noises, the tinkling clatter of elemental nature being tortured. Down near the spring branch were a number of 4-inch holes, perhaps where cows, drinking from the stream, had sunk into the mud in better days. First we chunked around in the icy holes with cornstalks stolen from the cows' hoard in the barn. Then we took golf swings, knocking the ice-encased dried grass flat to the ground, as our invisible golf balls soared over the pig pen.

Before Christmas we had a reason to go trekking in the woods—down to a holly tree on Fannie Early's place to get greenery to decorate the house; over into our own woods near the end of our property line to gather running cedar, for the same purpose. Often we would find a hornet nest high up in a tree in the woods. We had to have that, for every school kid then knew that teachers were just MAD for hornet nests to hang in the classroom. Larry and I didn't shoot guns, so sometimes we had to beg the help of our older brothers to get the nest down without essentially damaging it. They were the only ones who gathered mistletoe for Christmas, because it had to be shot down, a parasitic plant that grew high up in oak trees. Mistletoe was mostly poached from abandoned property, such as directly across from where the New Road branched to the left off of 604.

During clement winter days, we progued the woods kicking up the deep drifts of half-wet oak leaves in Uncle Ernest's woods. We made acorn pipes with the large brown nuts that the squirrels had missed. We scouted out stands of the smoky purple wild black raspberry canes that we would remember for next July. We cut little whistles of mountain laurel wood, green and pliable in the depths of winter. If all else failed, we could help Daddy do some work like burning old, dead weed stalks and minor brush, baking potatoes in the coals of the fire. We drank drafts of icy-cold water straight from the spring, sometimes in coconut shell dippers, feeling old-timey (one of Mama's favorite adjectives) and pioneering.

Part of the pleasure of a good snowfall was the making of snowcream. We scooped pristine snow off the top, usually in a metal bowl, added creamy milk, some vanilla, some sugar. God's own manna that fell from the skies.

With the advent of television at Uncle Ernest's, fall and winter Saturdays when we were in school lured Larry over there to keep the Unc company in watching football and, later, basketball—a new field for Larry's love of sports and statistics. I stayed at home, annoyed by football, and poked around for good reads. We always had a big selection of old magazines and pulpy fiction that relatives had given Daddy, and every now and then a racy joke book that Uncle Ernest's sons had given to Daddy. I'd curl up under a heavy quilt next to a sunny window in our unheated upstairs bedroom, isolated and content.

On long winter nights when our favorite cousins, the McDaniel girls, came over, we would play games at the dining room table—Setback, Rook, Michigan Rummy, all the while eating canned goods and cakes and pies if any were happening. We ate cucumber pickle, pickled peaches, sour cherries, applesauce, blackberries, and all canned goods our whims told us we wanted, even down to big jars of canned beets.

When Uncle Ernest's youngest child, Aubrey, took a sabbatical from Baltimore, if he came over on a winter night we generally played Setback or Keyword, the Scrabble-like crossword game that we thought superior to Scrabble. At Uncle Ernest's Aubrey taught us various kinds of poker, blackjack (21), and some rudimentary pinochle.

Left to our own devices on winter nights, Larry and I would play with Carl's Poosh-Em-Up pinball machine, getting right down on the cold linoleum floor of Mama and Daddy's bedroom to play mainly baseball and Put 'n' Take. One winter Sunday we found that the Richmond newspaper supplement published a Parker Brothers game that I think was developed by the noted author Hendrik Willem van Loon, Worldwide Travel. We loved it and didn't mind that we probably learned a little geography while playing.

Sometimes Mama would dig into her bag of winter cooking tricks and come up with something fitting for the time but not usually made. At night she might make some pancakes and bacon, though the syrup was not the super-expensive maple syrup but Karo corn syrup. Or she would whip up a fluffy omelet, which we never had for breakfast. She put baking powder in her omelets, something I've never heard of elsewhere. She would make a bit of nut brittle. We often grew popcorn and would have that on winter nights, shaking a cast-iron skillet back and forth on the wood stove. And, as mentioned in the food chapter, we fried potato and sweet potato slices right on the cast iron of the stovetop. Eating was our second job on winter nights. Our first was amusing ourselves.

As late winter finally slogged in, we heard, or fancied we heard, some susurrations of spring. In fields, especially in those formerly cultivated, Mama or Daddy would find the dark green of Upland Cress, always known as "cree salad" in our region. If cree salad came, could spring be far behind? It was our first taste of wild greens for a few months, and we relished it, especially with apple cider vinegar poured on.

On windy March days Larry and I would go to the few pin-oak trees that edged the top of the cow pasture near Uncle Ernest's woods. From this highest spot on our land we could see the full panorama of the Blue Ridge Mountains, the mingled hardwood and evergreen swoops of trees from the mountains to our land, the spiraling smoke from Mama's cookstove, which seemed to vibrate the air with an unheard hum. There we stood, and when the gusts came, driving the last of the leaves from the unyielding pin-oaks, we ran after them like crazed beings. We had to catch as many as we could before they hit the ground.

It would not be long now until the song of the unseen peepers would be a rackety chorus. We had come through.

Chapter 10

At William Monroe

When my sister Kay was in high school (class of 1956), she heard a member of a visiting athletic team ask, "Is that your school, or is that a chicken coop?" Probably his high school was 1950ish modern—all steel and glass and molded plastic. William Monroe, opened in 1925, at first with only a dirt floor in the basement, was no doubt physically dated in the mid-50s. Its auditorium doubled as half of a basketball court; its classrooms were sometimes jammed with bodies until William Monroe Elementary school was built, opening in 1954. When I first went to Monroe, one class, Miss Webb's fifth grade, had steps up to a large window to get into or out of the classroom, only one-half of a larger room, the library taking up the whole room again when the new elementary school opened.

William Monroe High School as it was in the 1950s.

The school originally had eight classrooms—one of these, sub-divided, used in my day as the school office and mailroom, the principal's office, and one small room doubling as a teacher's lounge and a mimeograph room. Going into that small room to get a volleyball once for the playground, I found the room a cloud of smoke as the teachers took a break. One of Kay's favorite teachers told her that I walked in just as the teachers were discussing what a fine family of students the Baughers were, so polite and attentive. The classrooms were situated around the perimeter of the main floor of the building, up half a flight of wide stairs from the entrance. Two more main classrooms were added to the back of the building after the initial eight, the one on the right end serving as the library. These classrooms surrounded an unsoundproofed auditorium/half of a basketball court. A bouncing basketball was part of an Algebra I class just as of Typing II.

Staircases on either side of the main half-flight of stairs going up to the classrooms were not strictly up or down, though the left one was preferred for going down to the basement, and the right one for up. At the left end of the basement the school lunchroom sat, its smells permeating the basement classrooms on the back of the basement area. The front side of the basement was made up of the coal furnace room and large girls' and boys' restrooms. Smokers hung out in the restrooms. The school had few athletic teams and no changing rooms or showers.

Still, I found the inside of the school warm and inviting, with character to spare. The wood floors, the huge windows, the high ceilings spoke of a serious edifice with a serious purpose. Out front, huge columns bespoke the serious purpose of the building. About half of the classrooms had an exterior door that let onto a wide and high staircase, two rooms sharing the small porch and staircase.

There's no way of proving my assumption, of course, but I would bet that the education we got at William Monroe was at least as good as the education that the rude young athlete got at his school, and probably better.

The greatest factor in any school's educational program is the quality of the teachers. We had many excellent ones; we had characters who left us with a store of memorable anecdotes; we had mentors that pushed us gently and imperceptibly toward what was right for us. For instance, I doubt that I would have gone to college at all—there was no money and no family tradition of that—had I not been nudged by Marguerite Stephens's just assuming that of course I would; by Laura C. Moyers's telling me that I was a born mathematician; by J. R. Breeden's finding out about the Granville Meade Scholarship and driving me to the interview, as proud as a father when I won one of the six Meade scholarships given in the state of Virginia, allowing me to go to college, paying about half of my expenses for the four years.

Let's go back a bit. I first went to William Monroe in September of 1953, entering the sixth grade of Ruth Tanner after going to Celt Elementary School through five grades in four years, all grades taught by Mary K. Towne in one room without electricity or water, with a wood-fired tin heater, so I know primitive. In that year, 1953, Celt was closed in the county-wide consolidation of schools. All eleven grades (becoming twelve grades before Larry and I graduated) were then contained in the one building, and it was full.

So when I was a month short of ten years old, I rode a school bus for the first time. Living near the start of our bus route, in Celt, only about seven miles from William Monroe, we had a long ride since the bus went up the New Road toward Dyke and returned and also up a road near the Gas Plant and returned. Our bus driver for my first three years at William Monroe, as I remember, was Abe Dulaney, Daddy's arch-enemy. I gave this watery-eyed late middle-aged man no trouble, and he gave me none. But he required that the first people on the bus go to the back and fill up gradually toward the front of the bus. In cold weather, a long bus's heating system scarcely reaches the back of the bus at all. On those cold days we got to the school with icy feet, but most of the classrooms were over-heated. On the bus, some kids kept warm by constant picking at each other and getting into fights.

In the next four years A. D. (After Dulaney), upperclassmen from William Monroe drove our school bus route: Donald Snow first, and then D. P. Chapman—both from up the New Road; and in my junior and senior years classmates Woodrow Shifflett and Elton McDaniel. They were mostly better drivers (perhaps not Woodrow) and not such sticklers for stacking students from the back seats forward.

We had but one teacher in the sixth grade, and Mrs. Tanner was as loving and lovable a teacher as I ever had, always joking and tossing puns around with students. But she was as serious as need be and ran a tight ship also. I was glad I had her, like some siblings before me, and not the other sixth-grade teacher, Helen Murphey [*sic*], who presided in a basement classsroom, not in one of the main classrooms, those surrounding the auditorium. Mrs. Murphey seemed likable but quite ditzy and frazzled most of the time. Harvey Peyton, the fraternal twin of Kennon, who was in Mrs. Tanner's class, had Mrs. Murphey. But Larry and I both lucked out and had La Tanner. Here we met classmates that became close friends and fellow graduates seven years later: George Lamb, Kennon Peyton, Wendell Lamb, Franklin Shifflett, Vivian Taylor, Arline Collins, Daphne Moyer, and Carolyn Jean Shifflett—the taller one, the blonde, Conrad and Elsie's daughter, not the reddish-haired other Carolyn Jean Shifflett in the same classroom. The students from Ruckersville did not come to William Monroe until the next year, for the seventh grade.

Ruth S. Tanner, who taught Larry and me in the sixth grade at William Monroe.

I often carried a big stack of books home with me, both class books and library books. This was before the day of backpacks, now almost universal. Wendell did me the kindness of telling me that as a boy I had to carry the books, no matter how big a stack, gripped in my hand by my side, at the end of my extended arm. Carrying books in both hands, my arms crossed over my chest, he informed me, was a girl's way of carrying books. I must never do it. I didn't want to embarrass my brother Roy, now in his senior year (11th grade then), or sister Kay, in the 9th grade, so I followed the gender rules that I was taught.

A number of students in each year's class would not be there the next year, whether moving or dropping out I did not know. The student that I remember best from Mrs. Tanner's sixth grade who was not there the next year in the seventh grade was Joe Snow, the chief sparring/joking partner of Mrs. Tanner. He questioned the reason for most tasks that he was set to, "What fer?" no doubt in part because it gave Mrs. Tanner the chance of saying "Cat fur to make kitten shoes."

When I look at Mrs. Tanner's report of my grades for the sixth grade, I see that of eight exams the first semester, the lowest score was 98 (ironically, in English); on the other seven exams I scored 100%. On my averages for the whole school year, five courses were 99%. No wonder I liked her so much.

In the seventh grade we changed classes and teachers for the first time, having three teachers. My homeroom teacher was Lewis Jollett, an old friend of Daddy and somewhat superannuated. He may have once been a better teacher than at that time of his life. He liked me and would grab me to talk to in idle moments. I could not be surly to him; but Larry could. He brought out the most stubborn wiseacre side of Larry, who, asked about some historical figure, I don't remember whom, told Mr. Jollett that he was the inventor of Jergens lotion. The man, retaliating for this snarkiness, I suppose, entered on Larry's report card that he had earned a semester average of F in Civics, though Larry had no marking period with a grade below a C. This was typical.

When I was a senior, I was a National Merit Scholarship Alternate Winner, which meant that all I got was the glory, no scholarship money unless some winner did not take the scholarship. Mr. Jollett told Daddy that somebody local—I don't remember who—had taken my scholarship from me and given it to another student. How could the man have gotten things so bollixed up, a clear impossibility to anybody but a conspiracy theorist?

Ruby Parrott was another of my seventh-grade teachers. Many students hated her and had horror stories to tell. Though she had a few weird facial movements and seemed a bit distant and inarticulate at times, I found her to be a good teacher, treating me warmly and fairly. Of course, I realized even then that I was so well-behaved and over-achieving a student that I don't remember having any teachers that disliked me or treated me unfairly. Mrs. Parrott unwisely stood on a folding chair to reach the top of our classroom Christmas tree and hurt her ankle and was out of commission for a short while. Our substitute teacher was usually a Mrs. Barnes (Lucille), an unfortunate alcoholic with broomstick legs. Of course, we tormented her and gave her hell. On the other hand, whenever I talked to Mrs. Parrott, she quirked up the side of her mouth and smiled at me.

The general favorite teacher in the seventh grade was Ida B. Deane, the mother of the business teacher Dorothy Lawson, a special favorite in later years. Mrs. Deane was also the aunt of one of the new Ruckersville students, Gayle Breeden. We did lots and lots of spelling in Mrs. Deane's class. I remember intramural spelling bees where the top two spellers, Vivian Taylor and I, got to pick sides. It ended up as virtually an all-girls team against an all-boys team. I suppose that most of the class thought that I was biased in picking non-shining students like Dickie Lamb, Kenny Teel, and Harvey Peyton for my side. But I was a close observer of all things academic, and I knew that these boys were all really good at spelling, though no shining lights in other subjects. As I remember it, my team handily won, but I admit that I don't really know. I was just thrilled by my inside knowledge of who the ringers were and my confidence in going with them.

Near the end of the seventh grade, in the spring of 1955, we had an all-school spelling bee on stage of the auditorium. Our seventh-grade spelling book would be the source of all words used, and Mrs. Tanner would be the one giving the words. She patted me on the cheek on stage before the curtain was drawn. I knew how to spell every single word in that book, but this was the first time I had ever been up on the stage, the first time I had ever been in front of so large an audience, a full house. I was so nervous I could barely speak. So on the second round, after spelling my word, "emperor," correctly, I changed it to "e-m-p-o-r-o-r." Mrs. Tanner said, "I'm sorry," and I slunk off the stage. Of course, my nickname for the rest of that school year and perhaps into the eighth grade was "Emperor," probably bestowed by George Lamb and Kennon Peyton, certainly used by them the most. I suppose it was a lesson worth learning. Many years later, teaching my first college class at Tulane University, I had to sit down at first to make sure my knees didn't quake. Soon I would stand up, peripatetic, rolling my -rs, and in general thinking that I could handle that. Indeed, the director of freshman composition, standing in the hallways, told me that I was no longer his worry, that I sounded like Billy Sunday up in the pulpit.

Mrs. Deane was a really good teacher, and I fondly remember her and honor her. Still, such is the perversity of human nature that my mind summons up mostly trivia, especially the perfectionist side of my human nature, always rampant. I remember her vividly for a stage performance, a school skit, where she was a nurse measuring a prone student's school spirit with a yardstick. Even more vividly I remember that Mrs. Deane thought that Pearl Harbor is in the Philippines, and spoke of it many times.

I never knew what to do when a teacher made an obvious mistake: Should I just grind my teeth and remain politely silent? Or should I come across as a smart-ass and correct the teacher, if only after class? The most egregious offender here was Hester Hall, my tenth-grade English teacher and sometime P. E. leader. She was idolized by most of the girls in the class, this short, broad, feisty woman who could spike a volleyball like a pro, telling us to "Roast the tater" instead of "Rotate." In English, she didn't seem all too fond of our British Novel of the Year, *Silas Marner*, like many of the students, and she drove us torturously through *Julius Caesar*, our Shakespeare for that year, the students who couldn't read Shakespeare dialogue still reading it. You haven't suffered Shakespeare torture if you haven't heard Kenny Teel call "Calpurnia! Calpurnia!" in a totally uninflected monotone with a deep Southern country accent.

Driving Kenny Teel to act was not Mrs. Hall's offense really. But she insisted on handing on Miss Grobyish nonsense about the English language. If a student used the word "kid," she'd respond, "A kid is a baby goat." I wanted to say, "Look in a dictionary, for God's sake. Every thinking person knows that a word can have more than one meaning. Even if you consider it slang, don't hand me this hokum as 'teaching proper English.'" Or she'd utter the prejudice that a word should be pronounced just as it's spelled. She would say that the word "again" should be pronounced "a.GAYN," again just spouting nonsense. Good luck on such a bias in pronouncing English. But I was too docile or, more likely, too chicken to say anything most of the time. Still, these are merely crotchets, and I admit that Mrs. Hall engaged the students and taught a mostly lively class.

In Mrs. Hall's English class we practiced the then-standard rigor of having students memorize great swaths of poetry. Once, one could expect to find that students everywhere in the region that were coevals had memorized the same passages of poetry: bits of "Rime of the Ancient

Mariner"; Wordsworth's "My heart leaps up . . ."; "Life is but a walking shadow . . ."— the longish speech out of MacBeth's desolation; poems by Philip Freneau and William Cullen Bryant; the General Prologue to Chaucer's *Canterbury Tales*, never mind that most of us mangled Middle English mercilessly; and Marc Antony's funeral oration for Julius Caesar— "Friends, Romans, countrymen . . . ." It is a very long oration. I thoroughly approved, and approve, of such an exercise, especially if it is coupled with the teacher's demonstrating the meaning of the language—the unctuous irony of Antony's calling Brutus an **honorable** man, the quiet demagoguery of Antony's maneuvering the thoughts of the mob. Not enough of this took place. Still, it was work well worth doing.

My homeroom teacher in the eighth grade and my English teacher, perhaps also my math teacher, was William S. Harrison, though he wrote his name on the report card as "Mr. Harrison" only. Mr. Harrison, or somebody that I cannot remember, gave me several A+s in math, and both semester exams are recorded as "100."

My 8th-grade school picture.

Dorothy Hood, I think, taught me eighth-grade history. She passed my little test: I asked her about the Dixiecrats in American politics, and she came back with an informed response.

Barbara Breeden Norcross, the daughter of the principal, J. R. Breeden, was my homeroom teacher in the ninth grade and, in the usual way of things, my English teacher that year. Until the last two years of high school English, each year's English literature was drawn from a big anthology which, as I remember, had a mix of American and English literature, heavy on the English. Our big work for that year's literature was *David Copperfield*, though perhaps somewhat abridged. She, like her father, had the knack of being a very good and knowing teacher while being quite easy, or so it seemed to me. At any rate, my report card—all of them kept at home and later by my sister June—shows my grades for the first three marking periods, the exam, and the first semester to be A+'s, as for the fourth marking period; and then I slacked off to mere A's.

My sophomore, junior, and senior homeroom teachers were Marguerite Finley Stephens, Nancy Hicks, and Esther Davis, though none of the three taught me English that year. In the junior year, though Mrs. Hicks was an English teacher, I had Vida Glass for that class, with the junior year being devoted, if I remember correctly, to American literature. Each year probably had literature as less than half of the semester's study, much devoted to grammar and usage and writing.

Which teacher I had which year and which readings were in which year may be slightly flawed or imperfectly remembered. But I am confident of what we studied, what poetry we memorized, which major works we read, what mis-teachings made up a small piece of our study, and of each teacher's style, especially for the English classes.

Our junior year English literature seemed to be mostly if not altogether American, as our senior year included only English literature. Mrs. Vida Glass was my English teacher that year, giving us the assignment, the first I had, of a long research paper, though I don't remember having any instruction in crediting sources or citing ANYTHING in footnotes or a bibliography. Since a young boy, I read, as a hobby, material on the history of the English language. (I know, nerdissimus.) So that's what I chose as the topic of my research paper, "This Strange Language." I remember that in one spot I quoted a bit of Old English, technically Old English, that is English before the Norman Conquest in 1066, not just olden English. Next to the passage, Mrs. Glass wrote, "Where did you find this?" I took this comment as her praising me for the diligence of my research. Only years later did I realize that she was asking about my source. Still, she gave me an A+ on the paper and said, "Thank you for this paper." No wonder I mistook the meaning of her query.

For senior English, we had the redoubtable Marguerite Finley Stephens. She was mostly the school librarian but at that time was the only one who taught senior English, the principal expressing the idea that only she did such a job that no one complained. In literature we did pretty much the standard curriculum of an English survey: parts of *Beowulf,* some of Chaucer's *Canterbury Tales,* memorizing the General Prologue, on through *MacBeth,* and so on. I can still remember Mrs. Stephens's rendering of Lady MacBeth's dialogue about nursing babes and smashing their brains out rather than failing to do what MacBeth had said he would do. "But screw your courage to the sticking point."

We did a good deal of writing, and it was well criticized. I remember especially an assigned paper of commentary on an editorial cartoon and another that was to be a character analysis drawn from Goldsmith's *She Stoops to Conquer.* She warned me not to parade my ostentatious vocabulary around when I got to college.

Marguerite Finley Stephens, who was the high school librarian and taught senior English.

The hardest part of any high school English course in those days was sitting still to listen to interminable book reports, the sixteenth retelling of the plot of *Pride and Prejudice*. I was sure that I would never read the work. If Darcy and Bingley had had any mercy on high school seniors, they would have left the Bennett girls alone. Little did I know then that the novel would later become perhaps my all-time favorite.

Mathematics was my other special love throughout school. Back at Celt Elementary I remember that one year Miss Towne apologized to me for having given me a math exam in either the fourth or fifth grade. We were excused from an exam in a course in which we earned all A's and B's. Almost nobody was ever excused from math exams, Miss Towne being a really rigorous grader.

In high school, I took Algebra I and II, both taught by Laura C. Moyers, the assistant principal and oldest teacher at the school. She was very hard of hearing and was sometimes thus the butt of student pranks, but—on the whole—a fine teacher and a good sport. She would wiggle down the close-packed rows of desks, this matronly figure of a woman, saying, "Make way! Make way! I'm not Miss Settle!" Miss Settle was one of the teachers at the school, she of the statuesque figure, who wore mostly sheath dresses and stiletto heels, though appearing every now and then in a skirt with crinolines beneath and ballerina flats on her feet.

Mrs. Moyers, the only Latin teacher at the school (but I couldn't take it when I tried, for there was not enough demand), would tell really bad jokes featuring dog-Latin. We could get her off topic by asking her opinion of some pop-culture-of-the-moment phenomenon. Of Elvis Presley, she said, "Hmph! Greasy hair and wet sideburns," which became one of our catch-phrases. She added, "Never did see anything to that Frank Sinatra either. All of that squealing from silly girls."

Laura C. Moyers, assistant principal and teacher of mathematics and Latin.

I would have liked to take trigonometry and calculus also, but the school was much too small to offer such treats. (There were only 31 students in my graduating class.) We did have Plane Geometry, an easy and thoroughly engaging class to me, taught by the principal, J. R. Breeden, He also taught our one course in chemistry. We lacked nearly all scientific equipment for any lab work in chemistry or biology. No physics courses were offered.

Esther G. Davis, the wife of Greene County's Commonwealth's Attorney, taught courses in General Science and Biology. I found her delightful, a thorough teacher who yet sprinkled A+'s all over my report cards. She, too, could be gotten off topic to talk about pop culture in this classic rock and roll period. She told us her favorite song was Al Hibbler's remake of "Unchained Melody," but she swept her listenings wide. She once referred to Elvis Presley's "All Shook Up" as "Come On, Sugar." She laughed as much at herself and Presley's muddy diction as the class laughed at her.

Esther G. Davis, who taught biology and general science;
my homeroom teacher my senior year.

Dorothy Deane Lawson, daughter of Ida Deane, taught typing and shorthand courses, patiently and thoroughly. I don't remember ever hearing any student say anything negative about her. I am forever glad to have had two years of typing: it has stuck with me, my keyboard skills probably sharpening with the years and always proving invaluable. Sometimes it was rough going, such as when we had to take our turns on the electric typewriter. Being heavy-fingered, I would sometimes get a whole shoal of unwanted characters. We had a number of different brands of typewriters. I remember only one electric one, an IBM perhaps. We had Royals, Smith-Coronas, Remingtons, and a couple of Underwood-Olivettis, huge slabs of heavy metal. We had to rotate on the machines and so experienced them all. We had more newish Royals than anything else, and I disliked them above all except perhaps the electric one. My favorite manual typewriters were all of the Smith-Coronas, but I liked the Remingtons well enough, and the Underwood-Olivettis, the oldest in the room, I liked nearly as well as the Smith-Coronas.

Some days, my accuracy in typing would just go haywire: I remember one 5-minute test of speed typing when I had 45 errors in five minutes! I don't remember my speed that day. Typing II seems to be the only course that I had at William Monroe where I got an A- for the year's average rather than a straight A or an A+. Po' me.

Mrs. Lawson talked me into also taking two years of shorthand, since I was still saying I was not going to college. She said that it would do me good and give me the possibility of being something like a "gentleman secretary" or court stenographer should I really not go to college. I was really good at shorthand, better than at typing. In my senior year she arranged for me to take a government civil service test. I earned a GS level ranking usually earned only by those with some college experience and was offered a job in Washington, D. C. working for the federal government after high school—my first full-time job offer, which, thankfully, I turned down. Anyway, I don't know what this 16-year-old would have done in a large city by myself.

Dorothy Deane Lawson, who taught me two years
of typing and two years of shorthand.

Both typing and shorthand were a boon to me when I did go to college, typing a great aid for writing the scads of papers required, then with my own blue Smith-Corona portable, and shorthand for note-taking in classes. When some classmate asked to borrow my notes the night before a big test, instead of saying, "No, you jerkface," I said, "See if you can read them," flashing my notes, nearly every word of them in Gregg shorthand and unfathomable. I still often use a bit of shorthand when I have to write something speedily. It lasts and lasts.

I was the only guy in the shorthand classes (two years of it). Most of the girls complained that the phonetic Gregg shorthand played havoc with their spelling, but I saw no difference. I did not always write my characters with the greatest accuracy, but I could always read the shorthand, partly relying on my knowledge of the language and typical wordings.

The final teacher that I want to single out here is Robert Hart, then a recent graduate of the University of Virginia in Charlottesville, who taught U. S. History my junior year and American Government my senior year. In those classes we had more discussion than in any other high school class. Woodrow Shifflett always chimed in with an opinion, whether strictly relevant to the question or not, welcomed by a chorus of "Woody knows!" from a few fun-loving boys in the class. Woody usually had no clue. Diane Deane, Gayle Breeden, and I always sat near each other in Mr. Hart's classes, joking and talking together, perhaps doing just a bit of flirting, shy as I was.

I did a long, long paper for each of Mr. Hart's courses, one on certain aspects of the Civil War for the U. S. History course. The most vivid detail that I remember is that one of my sources was a thick book from near the end of the nineteenth century. I'm not sure how it got to the school library. It described nearly every battle of the war as "quite sanguinary." Indeed. For American Government we did papers on the cultures of the rest of the world—I'm not sure why. I did a big chunk of southeast Asia. Ambitious as all get-out, I covered just about anything you'd want to know about the Philippines, Indonesia, Malaysia, Vietnam, Laos, Cambodia, Thailand, Burma, Tibet, and Bhutan. Hoo-boy! But I still remember a fair amount of what I learned.

Mr. Hart's rigorous tests always had at least one longer essay question. He refused to give anybody a 100% on any test, finding some little issue to deduct at least one point, saying that "Nobody's perfect." This galled me, for no one was claiming to be perfect by claiming that the single point was deducted wantonly, just so that the teacher could make a point. Still, my report card shows that my average for the YEAR in American Government is listed as A+.

Robert Hart, who taught me U. S. History and American Government.

And I know that Mr. Hart was as proud as could be of my academic skills. He was the teacher chosen to review students' test scores on the STEP (Sequential Tests of Educational Progress) and SCAT (School and College Ability Test) tests. I doubt that my classmates were unduly interested in the results of my tests, but Mr. Hart called me up to sit beside him at his desk as he loudly went over my results, forcing them to hear that, for example, on the SCAT tests, I scored between the 99th and 100th percentile on the verbal test and the same on the quantitative test. Apparently I was never left-brained or right-brained, neither side being dominant. (I still have the report, saved by June from the clothes hamper at home that I used to store my valuables in Larry's and my shared bedroom, so that I know my memory is accurate.) Mr. Hart let that little performance stand for hours of lecturing about the necessity of my going to college.

Success on standardized tests owed primarily to my second nerdiest enthusiasm that I had practiced for years: I had studied words for years, always taking the "It Pays to Increase Your Word Power" quizzes in *Reader's Digest,* not resting until I got a perfect score on every quiz, and inheriting from my sister June or buying for myself every book I could find on vocabulary-building, several of them by Norman Lewis or Wilfred Funk.

The verbal part of nearly every standardized test rests on knowledge of words and their meanings. Indeed, my job between my senior year of high school and my first year of college was achieved by performing well on the employment tests, almost altogether vocabulary tests in my day. I was offered a job at one of Baltimore's largest banks on the strength of such a test but could not assure them that the job was meant to be long-term. So I went to GMAC, the financing arm of General Motors, saying nothing about college—amazingly, I wasn't asked—and took the employment test, the same one I had had at the bank, confident that I got every single question right. One of my superiors at GMAC told me that I had scored higher on the employment test than any other employee ever there at GMAC of Baltimore. Arrogant little snip, I wasn't the least bit surprised, but I kept mum.

My high school principal, J. R. Breeden, had settled the issue of whether I was going to college or not the second semester of my senior year. There was no money, and Daddy had told me I couldn't go. I knew that his issue was mainly that he saw no way to get the money. But Mr. Breeden got me to apply for the Granville Meade scholarship, the regional one being one of six given in the state of Virginia. He even drove me to Charlottesville for the interview. Having no telephone, I found out that I had won the scholarship only when my father read it in the Charlottesville *Daily Progress.* He was clearly pleased at my achievement, saying, "I see you held their feet to the fire, Boot." I didn't know what he was talking about, nor why he was using his favorite pet name, usually reserved for Larry, of me; but I went to look over his shoulder and saw the good news.

J. R. Breeden, principal, who taught me Chemistry and Plane Geometry, and was instrumental in helping me to get a scholarship to attend college.

This scholarship would pay for about half of my expenses for four years at the college I chose to go to—Emory and Henry, in deep southwest Virginia, six hours away from home. The University of Virginia was only 20 miles from home, but I was determined to go farther away than that for college and establish my independence at a private liberal arts college with a strong reputation. I had not gotten any money for being an Alternate Winner of a National Merit Scholarship; most scholarships at Emory and Henry were tied to specifics such as being from a county nearby, being the child of a Methodist minister, etc., etc. But I would earn money by getting a summer job in Baltimore and working while in college. (I would eventually grade papers for five math professors and work at my dormitory desk the last two years of college.) To pay for most of the rest, I would take out a National Defense loan. No one but me would incur any responsibility for the debt, but the government required one's parents' signatures. I was sure that Daddy would balk, so I forged his name to the forms for the loan, repeating the forgery every year, with Mama's full knowledge. I could cancel up to half of the loan, for less than $2,000, ten percent of the loan for every year that I taught school at any level. And I had summer jobs to earn money, ranging from working on the frozen chicken dinner line at Morton Foods in Crozet, Virginia, to training to be a computer programmer at Potomac Edison in Baltimore, which did not work out.

I was later to find out that the Granville Meade scholarship was for men only and for whites only. I doubt that I would have had the strength of character to refuse to take it on moral grounds, so I'm glad I did not know at the time. My teachers had been right: I HAD to go to college.

The enclosed universe of high school, of course, involves more than academics. Most of my free time in high school was spent working, for free, in the library. Marguerite Stephens recruited me, instructed me, adopted me while at school as if I were her next-generation son. I fetched the mail for the library—including lots of incoming book orders—and spent many hours per week checking out books to other students, reading the shelves (Dewey Decimal system), and doing almost any job that Mrs. Stephens would normally do, especially when she had to go teach senior English when I was not a senior and was free to cover the library. The advantages added up, including getting first crack at the new books, learning a great deal about the books on the shelves, and getting to read just about every magazine that the library subscribed to, during idle moments at the check-out desk. I almost never had to sit through the tedium of study halls.

Other free times, such as in the morning before classes began and during extra time at lunch, much time was spent on playing games, sitting in folding chairs around the edges of the auditorium. Our school had very few discipline problems, and sweet-natured Principal Breeden and old softie Mrs. Moyers allowed such freedoms with no worries. We went through phases, different card games absorbing nearly all of our free time for days on end, Rook especially. We were nearly always allowed to play on the half-court for basketball there on the auditorium floor, so not just for the laughably inadequate Phys. Ed. courses.

I was not much good at sports of any kind, especially at basketball if I had to shoot overhand, not really being strong enough in my wrists and arms for any degree of accuracy. However, when allowed to shoot underhand I could hit the basket with fine accuracy. During certain times of year, a few boys would play a pick-up game of touch football out on the school grounds, not where the cinders from the coal furnace were dumped, for they were painful to land on. I was not terrible at touch football, for, though I could not throw well, I was a fast runner and a fair catcher of passes, so that I could make a touchdown occasionally.

One year my Phys. Ed. teacher was Mr. Lohr, an aged man who couldn't do much more than give us the rudiments of calisthenics and teach health. Because of schedules we had only four or five boys in his P. E. class, so we wouldn't have been able to do much in sports anyway. We also had very little athletic equipment other than balls, bats, and volleyball nets. I think I remember correctly that Hester Hall once taught a P. E. course that I was in composed of both boys and girls. At least I remember a number of volleyball games with both genders, Mrs. Hall teaching us the game. Near the volleyball net was a tetherball set, a la Napoleon Dynamite, and I logged a good amount of time on that almost skill-free game.

We had what we called monkeybars on a cinder path near the school, a tall and elaborate setup for maneuvers like skinning the cat, so long as one didn't mind straining muscles, unjoining joints, and getting cinder burns on one's limbs. My very slight weight, somewhere around 120 pounds then, made me pretty good at things like chin-ups and hand-walking across the bars.

High school picture when I was 14 or 15.

Robert Bowman, Irvin Shifflett, Franklin Shifflett, and Larry and I spent lots of idle moments hanging out near where the school burnt trash. We would find dozens of milk cartons from the lunchroom waiting to be burned, reclosing the lids and stomping on them to make a satisfying bang. Of course, we held mini-competitions to see who could be the loudest.

The only two official sports available when I was at William Monroe were baseball for the boys and softball for the girls. The school was too small to field teams for much else, and we had no showers or special facilities for other sports. The competition came mostly from the adjacent county high schools, such as Orange and Madison, or from small private schools such as Miller School, in Albemarle County, or BRIS—the Blue Ridge Industrial School, at St. George. My best friend toward the end of school, Sanford Estes, was a pitcher on the baseball team, coached by Sanford's father, Harold Estes, the VoAg and shop teacher, whom I had had for my one semester of "Agriculture" in the eighth grade. Most of our time was spent in the fairly good shop, doing woodworking or making other things, mostly of metal.

Clubs we had aplenty, though many did not do a great deal. I was part of the Student Council (student government) for two years, but we had very little power and consequently spent time learning how to run a movie projector and things like that. Many clubs were "future" clubs—FFA (Future Farmers of America, wearing blue jackets with gold emblems), perhaps doing more than most clubs; FHA (Future Homemakers of America); FTA (Future Teachers Association); Business Club; Science Club; Library Club (which I belonged to); the newspaper staff, "Monroe's Voice"; and the annual (yearbook) staff.

The newspaper was entertaining—a few mimeographed sheets mainly featuring articles on individual students and teachers, with things like "favorite song," "pet peeve," and "life ambition." Each year saw the production of a hardback yearbook by the annual staff featuring black-and-white pictures of the students, seniors to first-graders, club activities, sports events, and so on. The editor my senior year was Jeannette Dudding. It is of course fun to look back at those pictures and memories. From the vantage point of nearly sixty years later, of course the events look rather simple and idealistic.

Each school year had its rota of seasonal events. Classrooms were decorated for each holiday, mostly in the lower grades, mostly with drawings and cutouts on the walls and windows. We had school assemblies for the bigger holidays, often with skits or playlets. I appeared in one, entering the stage singing a seasonal song, nervous as a puppy. My favorite cousins, Mildred and Patricia McDaniel, entertained my siblings no longer in school by retelling how my mouth during the singing at the end of the skit was exaggeratedly O-shaped, not at all Glynn-like.

The two biggest events of the year were probably the staging of the senior play and Mayday. In our senior year we staged "Headin' for the Hills." I volunteered to do all of the posters advertising the play, freeing me from volunteering to appear and having to act in the play. I designed and made by hand all of the posters to be displayed, a task that required probably a whole week of every free moment down on the floor of my bedroom lettering and coloring, perhaps the most tedious job I ever did. My brother Roy had appeared in his senior play, but thank you, no; I didn't want to be on stage.

Mayday, including the pagan rituals of the smaller children weaving, unweaving, and reweaving streamers on the maypole, round and round and round and round and round, dancing to the bouncing music, took several hours of the school day. We did it up big-time, with princesses in fancy dress marching in to "Pomp and Circumstance" (recorded) and the elected May Queen ending the parade. My junior year, the Mayday that I remember best, Mary Powell was Queen of the May, dressed perhaps like the Statue of Liberty, perhaps not, but certainly reciting the Emma Lazarus poem on Miss Liberty's tablet: "Give me your tired . . . ."

The school was also the setting for entertainments at night, sometimes sponsored by the PTA, sometimes by the seniors intent on earning money for the senior class trip. In my brother Roy's senior year, he talked his way into getting MacWiseman, a wonderfully skilled early bluegrass musician, to appear. Wiseman told a slightly off-color joke about an escaped lion and the frantically fleeing man who "slid around" corner after corner fleeing the lion. Several parents were utterly scandalized, as though they had NEVER, NEVER, NEVER even heard the phrase "scared the shit out of me," never mind that Wiseman never used the phrase. Ah, innocent times, when so small a suggested obscenity could set the whole PTA and "decent" people into an uproar. I remember one woman's saying that she would never again be party to having "hillbilly" music at the school.

I don't know when the school lunchroom got up and running. It was not there in 1925, when William Monroe opened. In my day, school lunch tickets were $1.00 per week of five lunches. Very few people brought their lunches from home, one reason perhaps being that there were no refrigerators in which to store them. The lunches featured lots of government surplus food, such as canned grapefruit sections, and were rather dull affairs, though perhaps reasonably nutritious. We tended to have a fairly steady rotation of the same meals. For instance, every Thursday we had one hotdog on a bun, nearly always with mashed potatoes, seemingly alternating canned green beans and sauerkraut, always with plenty of onions and condiments available, with a half-pint of milk in waxed cardboard rectangular cartons. It didn't taste like Mama's home cooking and couldn't be doctored up enough to be good.

Once a week, Mrs. Morris—the head cook—made a big batch of peanut butter cookies, which WERE really good, always served with fruited red Jello. One could buy extras for a few cents per cookie. However, Mrs. Morris quit as head cook when she was ordered to serve seconds to students who wanted them.

Late in my school career, I did not buy lunch tickets, using the dollar a week to add to my stamp collection or to my collection of records from the RCA record club. When we got home about 3:30, there were always big pots of food keeping warm on the wood cookstove, so we ate our fill and then ate again for supper.

We had very little diversity in Greene County and therefore at William Monroe. We had a relatively low percentage of Negroes, with probably over 90% of the county's population being of European—mostly English, Scottish, and Irish—descent. We saw very little of people different from us. Although the Supreme Court had ruled in Brown vs. the Board of Education, in 1954, that American schools must be integrated "with all deliberate speed," Virginia, led by Senator Harry F. Byrd's policy of "massive resistance," had dragged its heels. William Monroe was still totally segregated when I graduated in 1960, and the county's population was still dropping, lower than it had been during the Civil War.

As graduation neared, I had been accepted at Emory and Henry, the college waiving its usual requirement that new students go for a personal interview. Everyone knew far ahead that I was to be the class valedictorian, so I needed to prepare a farewell speech. By that time, I really wasn't too much bothered by the prospect of speaking, though the choice of topic was worrisome. Mrs. Stephens advised me to choose a topic from current events. The U-2 incident, in which American reconnaissance pilot Francis Gary Powers, of Wise, Virginia, not so far from Emory and Henry, was shot down over Russia, was quite recent, and so I chose that. I was not a very politically aware boy at 16, though I thoroughly approved of the rather liberal politics of Pogo. Looking back, I'm rather startled by how mildly conservative my valedictory speech was. J. R. Breeden introduced me as the young man (I still felt distinctly like a boy) who was graduating with the highest average of any student in William Monroe's history. Full of confidence, I sailed through the speech without a stumble, my family, with just about all of them in attendance, proud as proud. In a picture from the occasion, I am glowing with a Norman Rockwellian aura.

Just after graduation night events, spring of 1960.

For some reason (psychological reluctance to leave the school I loved, maybe?) I seemed to be the last person except two of the faculty to leave the high school the night of graduation. One of my family's cars, perhaps Kay's, was waiting for me in the parking lot on the side of the school, next to the road to Celt. I decided to cut through a side classroom, the one where I had been taught English classes by Hester Hall and Vida Glass, to the shared staircase outside. As I entered the classroom quietly, I saw that the principal, J. R. Breeden, and science teacher Esther Davis were straightening up the desks and adjusting the blinds. They didn't see me. Mr. Breeden was crying softly, and Mrs. Davis, with her usual soft expression of wry bemusement, was asking "Why? What's wrong?" With voice thick with emotion, Mr. Breeden said, "I just hate to see the best class we ever had, leave." I was touched almost to tears myself and so made a bit of noise and scooted for the door.

Here's to that good class, all 31 of us: besides Larry and me, Gayle Breeden, Gene Collier, Arline Collins, Diane Deane, Lois Carol Deane, Lillian Dickerson, Jeannette Dudding, Carolyn Durrer, Sanford Estes, George Lamb, Wendell Lamb, Brenda Lillard, Elton McDaniel, Roy McDaniel, Lois Meadows, Doris Ann Morris, Faye Mowbray, Daphne Moyer, Harvey Peyton, Kennon Peyton, Alberta Shifflett, Carolyn Jean Shifflett, Franklin Shifflett, Patsy Shifflett, Woodrow Shifflett, Margaret Taylor, Vivian Taylor, Kenny Teel, and Jean Wright—13 boys, including 3 pairs of brothers—the Peytons and McDaniels and Baughers—and 18 girls, none of them paired with a sibling.

When we got home, we had a double celebration, of Larry's and my finishing that step of our life. Violet, of course, said, "I don't know how you could have had the highest average of anybody ever to graduate from Monroe. Mary Malone [valedictorian to Violet's salutatorian] had a 98-point-something average." I don't remember disputing the point, trusting that the school records were right.

Graduation night, celebrating the completion of this step of Larry's life and my life.

I suppose that I have done more than enough bragging on my academic accomplishments in this chapter. It is absolute fact, with documentation clear, but I could have dodged the facts. However, I mean to honor my teachers as well as myself. Had they not pushed and pushed, cajoled and argued, helped and gone many an extra mile for this naive, shy, and polite young boy, I would not have gone on to college and a career in college education. I would not have graduated first in my class at Emory and Henry College, with majors in my two loves, mathematics and English. I would not have won a two-year Woodrow Wilson Fellowship which paid in full for my first two years of graduate school, with an additional $1,000 per year for incidental expenses. I would not have gotten a teaching assistantship to pay for the rest of my graduate education.

Bit by bit, it all concatenated; and along the way no one ever asked whether I went to a chicken-coop school.

Mini-Epilogue

Looked at from the outside, my early life may seem deprived: my family did not have much of the material comforts America often affords. It was clear that we were po'. Still, it almost never felt so at the time, and now it feels like I had an early life of infinite riches.

I don't remember ever feeling anxious about life at large or the future to come. I wasn't oblivious, but I lived mostly below time, free of niggling worries, lassitude, and ennui. I had no philosophical bent, and the world wagged on.

The last of nine children, I never felt like one too many, nor like part of a group burden. Both of my parents seemed to have an infinite capacity for work for and love of their offspring, though one often could not perceive that love in my father, he of a deranged intemperance of temper. My mother was the warmest human being I've ever known. I never heard the too-easy expression of "I love you" from either of them. Yet who could doubt it?

Indulged by my family, my siblings especially, I was generally not spoiled. No one ever accused me of being so. Luckily, I was born bright, of two very intelligent though very slightly educated parents, and my Uncle Ernest, across the hill, was a kind of surrogate parent. My academic tasks were not irksome, and I was a very quick worker. Without straining myself in the least, I could earn A+s to sprinkle all around my report cards. Miss Towne had the insight to put me in the third grade once I turned seven, and thereafter I could be with my youth's second self, my crippled-with-shyness but delightfully insouciant brother Larry. He knew how to have fun.

I had a little world of relatives living nearby, enough to complement my life, not so many, or so close, as to press and meddle.

It was not a life to engender a sophisticate, a highly cultured person in touch with the grandeur of life, or an *artiste*. At any rate, such a person would have been considered to be "getting above his raisings."

From today's vantage point, I must consider my nearby neighbors, those within a quarter mile, to provide Austenesque comedy, a kind of quacking chorus. But they were mostly genial and generous, treating me with at least tolerance or indifference, and sometimes with admiration, never with hostility. They were nearly all ignorant of the world at large, in the most pristine sense.

In that time, in that place casual racism and religiosity were endemic. I grew out of the first, and the second never took. And when Emory and Henry College became my spirit-home, I slowly grew into the world.

Printed in the United States
By Bookmasters